Postcard History Series

Forgotten
San Diego

VICTORIAN DEPOT. The downtown Santa Fe Depot seen in this 1912 postcard was built in 1887. Originally the California Southern Railroad Depot, the Victorian-era station was located at Broadway and Pacific Highway (originally D and Atlantic Streets). It was demolished in 1915 after a new, much larger Spanish Revival–style depot was constructed across the tracks to handle the crowds headed to visit the Panama-California Exposition in Balboa Park. (Courtesy of the David Marshall postcard collection.)

ON THE FRONT COVER: WONDERLAND. Most San Diegans have never heard of Wonderland Amusement Park. This elaborate entry, flanked by onion-domed towers, welcomed visitors to Wonderland. Located in Ocean Beach, south of Voltaire Street, between Abbott Street and the beach, Wonderland opened on July 4, 1913, to a crowd of more than 20,000 people. Occupying eight acres, the park boasted 40 attractions, including a dance pavilion, bowling alley, animal menagerie, roller-skating rink, seawater plunge, and fun zone. Despite its early success, Wonderland lasted only two seasons as attendance plunged with the opening of the 1915 Panama-California Exposition in Balboa Park. In 1916, high tides and winter storms damaged the park and later forced its permanent closure. (Courtesy of the David Marshall postcard collection.)

ON THE BACK COVER: BIG SCREEN. Cinema 21 had its gala premiere on July 19, 1963. The first film was *55 Days at Peking*, a historical war epic starring Charlton Heston. The modern-style theater included a semicircular glass lobby, a large Cinerama screen, and a seating capacity of 1,000. Located in the heart of Mission Valley, the theater was easily seen and accessed from the Interstate 8 expressway. After closing in 1998, the building served as a church and later a sporting goods store before being demolished and replaced by condominiums. (Courtesy of the David Marshall postcard collection.)

POSTCARD HISTORY SERIES

Forgotten San Diego

David Marshall, AIA, and Eileen Magno, MA

ARCADIA
PUBLISHING

Published by Arcadia Publishing
Charleston, South Carolina

Printed in the United States of America

Library of Congress Control Number: 2023935100

For all general information contact Arcadia Publishing at:
Telephone 843-853-2070
Fax 843-853-0044
E-mail sales@arcadiapublishing.com

Visit us on the Internet at www.arcadiapublishing.com

*David Marshall dedicates this book to his wife, Stacy; his family;
colleagues at Heritage Architecture & Planning;
and everyone who preserves historic buildings.*

*Eileen Magno dedicates this book to her husband, Jun,
and their children, Jon, Justin, and Ella; her mom, Cecilia;
the Heritage Architecture & Planning family;
and to all San Diego preservation advocates, archivists, and historians
who keep our community's history and memories alive for future generations.*

Contents

Acknowledgments

The authors would like to thank Roger Showley, Bruce Coons, M. Wayne Donaldson, and Stacy Marshall, who offered their proofreading skills and knowledge of San Diego history to help make this book as readable and accurate as possible. Also, thanks to Caitrin Cunningham, senior title manager, Arcadia Publishing. And finally, thanks to the San Diego History Center, the Coronado Historical Association, the San Diego Air and Space Museum, the Oceanside Historical Society, and the *San Diego Union-Tribune* archives, whose websites and staffs provided invaluable information about San Diego County's unique history. All images used in this book are from David Marshall's personal collection.

For the creation of *Forgotten San Diego*, every effort was made to reference primary sources, oftentimes by directly quoting the postcards themselves. Words in quotations were taken from a historical source. This book is our modest contribution to help keep San Diego's history alive—and not forgotten.

INTRODUCTION

There are places I'll remember, all my life, though some have changed,
some forever, not for better, some have gone and some remain.

—"In My Life," Lennon-McCartney, 1965

This book is intended to be a celebration of the history of San Diego and its neighboring cities as seen in the postcards of the time. This is a chance to see where we've been and better understand how we got here. While *Forgotten San Diego* was not written to be a sad remembrance of the places that we have lost, it's difficult not to miss these things from our past. Coauthor David Marshall's wife, Stacy, who proofread this book, lamented, "We had so many fun places that are now gone." The good news is that we can still keep those buildings, places, and experiences alive in our memories—and books.

Collecting postcards has become a popular hobby for history lovers. The cards depict our past with picturesque images and often carry postmarks that capture the date. Postcards also show what was deemed important in the past. If a place or event was important and worth remembering, postcards were made so the images could be shared with friends or mounted in a scrapbook. One must remember that, in the days before smartphones, most people didn't have a camera in their pocket wherever they went. In fact, prior to the 1940s, most people didn't even own a camera, so they relied on professional photographs on postcards to help document their towns and travels.

While some prefer to have pristine, unused postcards, the authors appreciate the cards that have handwritten messages and the addresses where they were sent. Sometimes, the messages are more interesting than the pictures. One of the most appealing aspects of old postcards is that they are actual artifacts from history, like antique furniture or vintage books. A collector knows that a Balboa Park postcard from 1915 with an exposition postmark was actually at the fair.

In the United States, penny postal cards were approved by Congress in 1898 and were used initially for advertising. Unlike later postcards, writing was not permitted on the back of a postcard until 1907. Only the address was allowed on the stamp side. For this reason, the oldest postcards often have brief messages crowded on the picture side of the postcard. In about 1900, real-photo postcards began to appear. Unlike colorized lithographed postcards, real-photo cards were black and white or sepia with much sharper images. Since real-photo postcards were actual, unaltered photographs, they grew in popularity and are still a favorite of collectors. Upwards of 75 percent of the postcards sold in the United States were printed in Germany and other European countries, where lithography was of higher quality than what the United States could produce. "The Golden Age of Postcards" is considered 1907–1915. In 1908 alone, Americans mailed over 677 million postcards, even though the US population was under 89 million.

The coauthors of this book are colleagues at Heritage Architecture & Planning, a firm that specializes in preserving and restoring old buildings as well as researching and writing about their history. All but two of the 213 images used in *Forgotten San Diego* are historical postcards from 1890 through 1990. They were selected by the authors to represent the best of what has faded from our collective memories. The images herein do not represent the full history of San Diego County, because postcards seldom highlight news events or social issues, but we think that you will find a good representation of the San Diego region and its history.

While selecting the images to include in this book, the authors combed through over 4,000 postcards to find images that were interesting or unique and had fascinating stories behind them. Many times, we discovered historical tidbits about the postcards that were surprising and sometimes shocking. One example is how two warships based in San Diego had tragic mishaps 39 years apart, and both ships had the identical name (page 24). And when the history of an unassuming ice rink led us to the "King of Rock and Roll" (page 87). Sometimes, the deeper you dig, the more treasures you find.

In *Forgotten San Diego*, you will not see some of San Diego's famous sites like the Belmont Park roller coaster or Cabrillo Bridge because they are—thankfully—still here. Those landmarks are not gone, nor are they forgotten. What you will see are beautiful buildings that you never knew about, fun places that you wish you could enjoy, and stories about San Diego County that will surprise you.

We hope that everyone enjoys this postcard compilation and takes away a better understanding of how present-day San Diego came to be. The saying goes "You don't know what you've got 'til it's gone." We sincerely hope that those who read this book, whether they live in San Diego County or not, will be moved enough to be vocal participants in their city or town and will help preserve what makes their home a special place. Let *Forgotten San Diego* serve as a reminder that we all must protect and preserve the best of what we have before it becomes history.

One

Ever-Changing City

Seashells by the Seashore. This vintage postcard was mailed in 1905 and shows a very early skyline of "New Town" San Diego. Few buildings were taller than three stories. While the wreath of seashells was an appropriate nod to San Diego's coastal location, this design was recycled by the postcard company for many other cities simply by changing the center image and caption.

FATHER HORTON.

FATHER OF SAN DIEGO. Alonzo Erastus Horton (1813–1909) founded modern San Diego. Born in Connecticut, he joined the Gold Rush in California in 1851. Horton moved to San Diego in 1867 and bought 960 acres along the waterfront for $4.26 an acre. This settlement became known as "Horton's Addition" or "New Town." San Diego had previously been established along the San Diego River in what is now Old Town. But Horton gambled on relocating the city's center closer to the bay and its shipping industries. A firm believer that the city should have a public park, in May 1868, Horton helped establish 1,400 acres for City Park—later renamed Balboa Park. This postcard photograph was published in 1908, one year prior to Horton's death at the age of 96.

San Diego Bay, San Diego, Cal.

A GROWING CITY. Overlooking Midtown and San Diego Bay in the early 1900s, this postcard reads "San Diego is the second largest town in Southern California and is noted for its climate the most even in the world. It has the finest landlocked harbor on the coast and is rapidly becoming an important commercial city." The Middletown Grammar School, constructed in 1888, is the large building with a tower. (For a better look at the school, see page 110.)

Portion of San Diego Business District, the Bay and Coronado Island, San Diego, Cal.

COPYRIGHTED 1911 BY ARCADE VIEW CO.

HOTEL DEL CORONADO

CORONADO ISLAND

TORPEDO BOAT STATION

BUSINESS DISTRICT. Published in 1911, this postcard was printed in anticipation of the 1915 Panama-California Exposition in Balboa Park and shows how the city has continued to grow. This aerial view shows the downtown business district south of Broadway. In Coronado, the Hotel del Coronado and the torpedo boat station can be seen.

SAN DIEGO 1915 EXPOSITION, NOW BUILDING

WARSHIPS COALING IN SAN DIEGO HARBOR

SAN DIEGO *The* HARBOR OF THE SU PANAMA CANAL ¶ HO

Ninety thousand population.

One of the best natural harbors of the world.

Building permits in 1912 were $10,001,415.

Fifty-four churches.

$150,000 Y. M. C. A. Building.

57 hotels, two of which cost $3,500,000.

Finest all-the-year climate in the world.

Doubled in population in the last three years.

Averages only three days in the year without sunshine.

A mean variation in temperature of eight degrees, summer and winter.

11 banks; capital $2,500,000; deposits $21,000,000.

Raised $4,800,000 for development purposes in one year.

PUBLISHED BY THE CHAMBER OF COMMERCE OF SAN DIEGO COUNTY.   FOR

NEW METROPOLIS OF THE PACIFIC COAST. This folding postcard was published by the Chamber of Commerce of San Diego County in 1912 as part of the campaign to boost the region ahead of the 1915 Panama-California Exposition. Photographs depict San Diego as a growing and thriving city,

N DIEGO—THE NEW METROPOLIS OF THE PACIFIC COAST

MESSAGE	ADDRESS

FIRST PACIFIC PORT OF CALL FROM THE F THE 1915 EXPOSITION, NOW BUILDING— HAS

Purest and cheapest mountain water in any city of America.
500,000 acres of unimproved land in back country.
Sufficient water conservable to irrigate every acre of valley land.
23 theatres, one of which cost $1,000,000, and is finest west of Chicago.
200 manufacturing industries.
City library containing 50,000 volumes.
Three daily newspapers and many weekly and monthly publications.
Aero Club, with the largest and finest aviation field in the world.
Curtiss and Army and Navy Aviation Schools, flying every day in the year.
Outdoor amusements all the year round: hunting, fishing, baseball, tennis, polo, swimming, yachting, motor-boating, rowing, golf, and autoing.

INFORMATION ADDRESS THE SECRETARY, WILLIAM TOMKINS, SAN DIEGO, CAL.

including a rare image of the exposition buildings under construction (upper left). The postcard calls San Diego "the Playground and Homeland of America," boasting 11 banks, 54 churches, 57 hotels, 23 theaters, and being the first Pacific port of call from the soon-to-be-completed Panama Canal.

Dear Mary - Sweet card received. Will write soon. With much love. Papa.

Fifth st. looking South, San Diego, Cal.

FIFTH STREET IN 1906 (ABOVE) AND 1909. Fifth Street (now Avenue) in downtown San Diego rose to prominence when Alonzo Horton built a wharf and started to develop the surrounding area. Fifth Street served as the commercial backbone of what is now the Gaslamp Quarter. Streetcar tracks were first laid along Fifth Street in 1886 by the San Diego Streetcar Company, owned by Coronado developers Elisha Babcock and Hampton Story. In 1892, the company was purchased by John D. Spreckels and incorporated into his San Diego Electric Railway. The entire 16-mile system would eventually be converted to electric operation by 1897 with the Fifth Street line being the first to be electrified. Streetcar No. 54 can be seen in the above image in the foreground. Miraculously, this car has survived and is on display at the San Diego Electric Railway Museum at the National City Depot.

413 – FIFTH STREET, LOOKING NORTH FROM F, SAN DIEGO, CALIFORNIA.

THAT SUNNY SPOT. Even before San Diego was promoted as the site for the 1915 Panama-California Exposition, the city was known for its sunny, temperate climate, as can be seen in the 1908 postcard above. Upon closer inspection, the center of the sunny spot is actually closer to Los Angeles. Sure enough, research revealed that both Los Angeles and Long Beach were promoted with nearly identical postcards, with only the text changing. Bruising San Diego's civic pride further, this same postcard was used to celebrate the National Democratic Convention of July 7, 1908, in Denver, Colorado, with the "sunny spot" appropriately shifted northeast. The c. 1940s postcard below, sponsored by Ye Golden Lion Tavern on Fourth Avenue, provides more detailed weather statistics regarding the climate in San Diego, also known as "America's natural air conditioned area." Prior to the impact of climate change, downtown San Diego averaged only one day per year where the temperature exceeded 90 degrees. Between 2014 and 2022, San Diego averaged six days per year above 90 degrees.

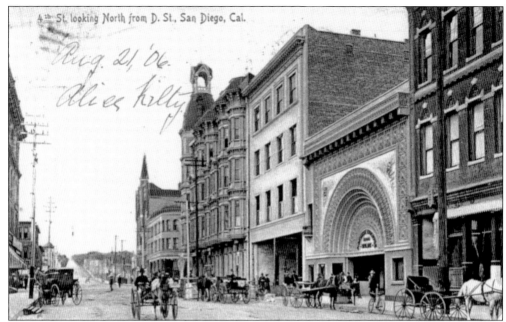

BUGGY TRAFFIC. Fourth Avenue is pictured from D Street, now Broadway, in 1906 without a single automobile in sight. The dramatic arched facade is the Pickwick Theatre, which was designed by architects William Hebbard and Irving Gill. The venue opened in 1905 as a vaudeville theater with seating for 825. It became a motion picture theater in 1922 but was demolished only four years later.

BIRD'S EYE. This c. 1920 aerial view of downtown shows the view from Market Street north to Balboa Park and the Cabrillo Bridge. The large white wall at the far left is the Spreckels Threatre Building. The U.S. Grant Hotel is two blocks to the right. Missing from this view is the El Cortez Hotel, which was not built until 1927.

4180. "D" Street on a busy Day, San Diego, Cal.

BUSY DAY. The primary east-west street in downtown San Diego was D Street. In anticipation of the 1915 Panama-California Exposition, local leaders decided to rename the street Broadway to sound more metropolitan. At the same time, the numbered streets, like Fifth Street, were all renamed avenues, but only up through Twelfth. The 1911 postcard above shows a bustling D Street looking northeast with the U.S. Grant Hotel in the distance. The c. 1920 image below shows D Street looking southwest with Horton Plaza Park framed by palm trees. To the left are buildings that once lined Plaza Street, including the Cabrillo Theater. The street was closed and the buildings were demolished in the early 1980s to make way for the Horton Plaza shopping mall.

4527 PORTION OF THE BUSINESS SECTION, CORONADO, NORTH ISLAND

AND POINT LOMA IN THE DISTANCE, SAN DIEGO, CALIF.

104518

A Glimpse of SAN DIEGO, Cal., from the Park.

GLIMPSE FROM THE PARK. This c. 1905 postcard shows an early view downtown from the western edge of City Park. In 1868, about 1,400 acres on the edge of downtown were set aside to create this park. In 1910, the city wanted to find a more compelling name than City Park. Harriet Phillips's suggestion of "Balboa" was chosen to honor the famous Spanish explorer Vasco Núñez de Balboa.

MATURING SKYLINE. This is a similar vantage point 60 years later, in about 1965, from behind what is now the San Diego Air and Space Museum in Balboa Park. In the foreground are the State Route 163 and Interstate 5 freeways. One of San Diego's earliest high-rises, the El Cortez Hotel, still tops the rest. Within 10 years, the skyline will be dominated by new bank towers.

MISSION VALLEY FARMLAND. Before a tangle of freeways and countless hotels took over Mission Valley, it was a thriving agricultural region beginning with the founding of the San Diego Mission and Presidio in 1769. Later farms were intensively cultivated, producing tons of vegetables each year. Dairy farms came in the 1880s, and by 1950, Mission Valley had 20 dairy farms. Several farmhouses and windmills can be seen in this 1910 image.

SQUARED CIRCLE. The development of Mission Valley began to take shape following World War II. The creation of Hotel Circle was spearheaded by Charles H. Brown, a local developer who constructed the first hotel in the valley, the Town and Country Resort, in 1953. The site included a 46-room motor inn. Other hotels soon followed within a mile of one another along service roads on either side of Interstate 8. Hotel Row would have been a more accurate name, but Hotel Circle was catchier.

ATOP THE MESA. Founded in 1897, San Diego State University began as the San Diego Normal School, a training facility for secondary and primary school teachers. In 1931, the student body and staff moved into a seven-building campus with an 11-story bell tower overlooking Mission Valley, seen above. Four years later, the school expanded its degree programs and became San Diego State College. By 1960, the school became part of the newly created California State University system.

SMOKE STACKS. Mills and power plants are seen in this smoky view from the corner of Eighth and L Streets in 1910. In 1881, the San Diego Gas Company was established and built its gas plant at Tenth and M Streets (now Imperial Avenue). Three miles of gas mains were constructed and 25 streetlamps were illuminated. Meanwhile, the first electric plant in San Diego, located at Second and I Streets, began operating in March 1886.

NO ORANGES. Orange Avenue in Coronado stretches one mile from bayside Coronado to the Hotel del Coronado. The avenue got its name from the orange trees that were planted in the center median in 1886. Unfortunately, wild jackrabbits also enjoyed the fruit trees, consuming them before they could mature. The remaining trees had to be uprooted, but the name stuck. This c. 1910 postcard shows only palms and trolley tracks in the median, with the Del in the distance.

EARLY LA JOLLA. Although La Jolla became incorporated as part of San Diego in 1850, no permanent settlers arrived until 1870, when Charles Dean acquired several of the pueblo lots and subdivided them into an area called La Jolla Park. In 1887, speculators Frank T. Botsford and George W. Heald laid out the community. By 1900, La Jolla had grown to 100 buildings with 350 residents. This postcard, looking west from Mount Soledad, shows that early period. The intersection at center-right appears to be Torrey Pines Road at Prospect Place when they were just dirt roads.

DOWNTOWN LA MESA. Lookout Avenue (now La Mesa Boulevard) and the Hotel Dorothy are seen in 1911. Pioneer movie director Allan Dwan, whose career spanned the birth and growth of the motion picture industry, was a frequent occupant of this La Mesa hotel early in his career. While in town he would film at an open-air lot in the heart of downtown. It is said that over 100 one-reel movies were produced in La Mesa by Dwan in 1911 alone.

STREET NAME SHUFFLE. Oceanside's Hill Street was officially part of Highway 101 and was the main route from Los Angeles to San Diego for many years. Highway 101 was rerouted to the east in the late 1940s and was eventually renamed Interstate 5 in the 1960s. In 1998, Hill Street was renamed Coast Highway to recall its connection to the historic Highway 101. In yet another street name change, Second Street is now Mission Avenue.

Two

MILITARY TOWN

US NAVAL TRAINING STATION. In 1917, the United States entered World War I and the US Navy took over Balboa Park's former exposition grounds to create San Diego's first naval training station. By 1918, up to 6,000 sailors at a time, averaging 19 years old, trained in the park. Here, soldiers are marching in the Plaza de Panama with the House of Hospitality in the background.

"Navy-Town" U.S.A. San Diego's reputation as a "Navy Town" is memorialized in this postcard from the 1960s. The aircraft carrier seen here is the USS *Bennington* (CV-20), which was commissioned on August 6, 1944, and later modernized. In 1954, a tragic catapult explosion and fire killed 103 men and injured another 200. Accidents like this eventually led the Navy to replace hydraulic catapults with the steam-driven systems still in use today. In 1970, the *Bennington* was decommissioned and sent to Bremerton, Washington. The ship was eventually sold for scrap in 1994 and towed to India.

U. S. Gunboat Bennington, two hours after Explosion in San Diego Bay, July 21, 1905

USS *Bennington*. Coincidently, an earlier ship named *Bennington* had its own tragic history. The USS *Bennington*, a 1,700-ton gunboat of the Yorktown class, was commissioned in June 1891. At 10:38 on the morning of July 21, 1905, a boiler explosion violently shook the ship on San Diego Bay, and large volumes of steam and ash filled most of the living compartments and deck areas. Of the 112 on board, 66 officers and crew were killed, and the *Bennington* never sailed again. A 60-foot-tall granite obelisk dedicated to the *Bennington*'s lost sailors can still be seen at Fort Rosecrans National Cemetery.

NAVY FLAG. Another view of the US Naval Training Station in Balboa Park, this c. 1918 photograph was taken from the California Tower looking east, showing several thousand sailors trying their best to clearly spell "NAVY" in the Plaza de Panama. The building at the center-left is the Home Economy Building, demolished in 1963. It is now the site of the Timken Museum of Art.

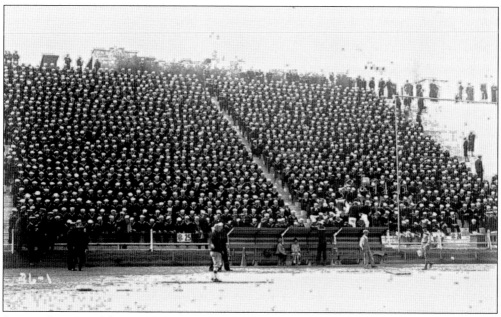

SAILOR STADIUM. The US Navy's occupation of Balboa Park in 1917–1919 included Balboa Stadium, originally called City Stadium. In this postcard, bluejackets fill some of the 15,000 seats at one of the largest municipal stadiums in the country at the time. President Wilson spoke at the stadium in 1919. Several years later, flier Charles Lindbergh celebrated his successful transatlantic flight with thousands of well-wishers at the stadium.

FORT ROSECRANS. Camp Wright was established on the western side of Point Loma's Ballast Point in 1852 and decommissioned in 1863. Fort Rosecrans was established in 1899 near the site of the Spanish Fort Guijarros, which was created in the late 1700s. It was named after Maj. Gen. William S. Rosecrans. Coastal defense fortifications were constructed in 1891–1903 and 1941–1943, and the base was transferred to the US Navy in 1957 as a submarine support facility. In 2023, the site is home to Naval Base Point Loma.

TARGET PRACTICE. Artillerymen in 1910 practice firing 10-inch-diameter mortars from the hills of Point Loma. In the 1920s, twelve-inch mortars were installed. By 1952, construction began on the Arctic Submarine Laboratory, located beneath the battery. The Naval Electronics Laboratory was designed during the Cold War to test the effects of Arctic ice, seawater, and water pressure on materials and devices intended for use by submarines. The Arctic success of the famed submarine USS *Nautilus* can be traced to the pioneering work conducted here.

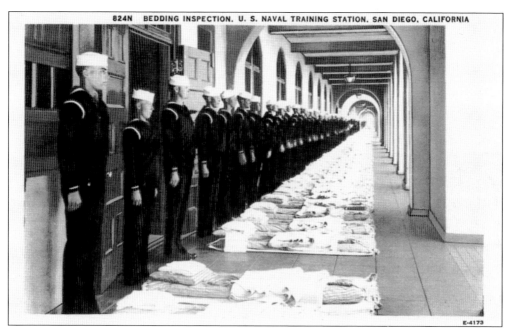

E-4173

INSPECTION TIME. These recruits are lined up for bed inspections at the Naval Training Station/ Center (NTC) in Point Loma around 1935. NTC was an active military recruiting and training center from 1923 to 1997 where 2.75 million Navy recruits and sailors were trained. In 2023, the decommissioned base is a historic district known as Liberty Station, with the old Navy buildings repurposed for restaurants, retail, arts, and culture.

"USS NEVERSAIL." Over 50,000 recruits per year learned basic naval procedures on this two-thirds-scale destroyer escort, a land-bound ship sailing on a sea of concrete. Commissioned on July 27, 1949, the USS *Recruit* was the Navy's only commissioned ship that never touched the water. It was nicknamed "USS Neversail" by recruits. The plywood ship was outfitted with standard naval rigging and even had a three-inch gun (but no ammo). It was the first of three mock ships built by the Navy for training after World War II, and it is the only one that remains. In 2004, the USS *Recruit* was designated a California historical landmark.

SUBMARINE *GRAMPUS*. The US Navy submarine the USS *Grampus* is pictured on San Diego Bay in 1913. It was a tiny vessel, only 63 feet long and 11 feet on the beam. Called the "demon divers" by early admiring San Diego newspapers, these submarines could only submerge to 60 feet. In 1915, the USS *Grampus* served in the Philippines, where it patrolled the waters off Manila during World War I. After being decommissioned in 1921, the USS *Grampus* performed its last military service as a target and was unceremoniously sent to the bottom of Manila Bay.

USS *SAN DIEGO*. The USS *California* was launched on April 28, 1904, and was renamed USS *San Diego* in 1914. The ship was a Pennsylvania-class armored cruiser. It was the only major warship lost by the United States in World War I, having been sunk off the coast of New York on July 19, 1918. Miraculously, only six lives were lost of the 1,183-man crew. In 2018, investigations of the wreckage revealed that the USS *San Diego* had been sunk by a German U-boat mine.

DUFFY THE DOG. The tenacious fighting of the Marines during World War I earned them the nickname "Teufel Hunden" or "Devil Dogs." Soon the image of the bulldog was embraced by the public and became the much-loved mascot of the Marine Corps. In 1939, the first official mascot of Marine Corps Recruit Depot San Diego was James Jolly Plum Duff. Duffy earned the rank of sergeant and served as the depot mascot until his death on May 15, 1945. This postcard was mailed from Camp Pendleton in 1943.

RECRUIT DEPOT. The Marine Corps Recruit Depot (MCRD) was established in 1919 on a 232-acre tideland known as Dutch Flats. In 1923, the area was formally commissioned by Gen. Joseph Pendleton. The original buildings were designed by architect Bertram Goodhue, who had previously overseen the design of the 1915 exposition buildings in Balboa Park. The base became the primary Marine recruiting center on the West Coast and remains an active military installation in 2023.

LA JOLLA'S CAMP CALLAN. The pre–World War II "Blitz Boom," as the *Saturday Evening Post* called it, saw the rapid expansion of military bases and camps. The US Army officially opened Camp Callan in early 1941 as a training facility and defense base. Located on 710 acres along the picturesque coastline of La Jolla, Camp Callan provided an ideal setting for soldiers to train for coastal defense operations. Due to the dangers of gunnery practice, swimmers and surfers were only allowed to enter the nearby waters on weekends.

South Entrance, Camp Callan.

WELCOME TO CAMP CALLAN. This 1943 postcard shows the south entrance to Camp Callan. About 15,000 men went through a 13-week training cycle specializing in coastal artillery and anti-aircraft defense weapons. The camp was declared surplus in November 1945 with most of the buildings being purchased by the City of San Diego and sold for salvage.

ABOVE CAMP CALLAN. A 1943 aerial postcard view shows some of Camp Callan's 297 buildings, which included three theaters, five chapels, and five post exchanges. The camp was named after Maj. Gen. Robert Callan, a distinguished US Army coast artillery officer and a veteran of the Spanish–American War and World War I.

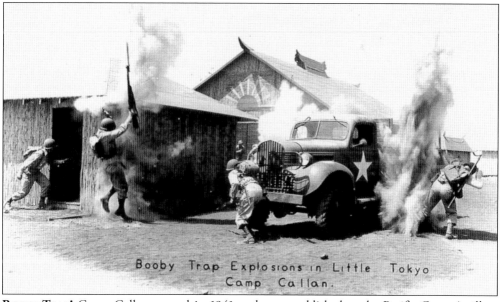

Booby Trap Explosions in Little Tokyo
Camp Callan.

BOOBY TRAP! Camp Callan opened in 1941 and was established as the Pacific Coast Artillery Replacement Center. The Army built the camp to train soldiers, and it opened less than one year before the United States entered World War II. By 1942, the camp included an infiltration course, grenade course, and mock training village known as "Little Tokyo," seen here. Today, the former base is home to the Torrey Pines Golf Course, the state reserve, and the campus of the University of California San Diego.

FIELD ARTILLERY. CAMP KEARNY, CAL.

KEARNY ARTILLERY. Camp Kearny was a desolate-looking area utilized as an Army infantry training camp during World War I. The area is now home to the communities of Linda Vista and Miramar. During World War II, the Navy made the southern part of the camp an auxiliary air station for North Island. In 1952, the northern portion became Naval Air Station Miramar. In 1969, the US Navy Fighter Weapons School ("Top Gun") was established there. The base transitioned into Marine Corps Air Station Miramar in 1999.

ARMY ONIONS. Gas masks and protective clothing were a critical part of the training process for soldiers in 1919, as World War I saw the first large-scale use of chemical weapons. The gas masks used by soldiers consisted of a face mask and respirator. Here, Camp Kearny soldiers from the 40th Division of the US Army cleverly utilize their training equipment for other, more immediate purposes.

Three

Parks and Amusements

4725. The Chutes, Wonderland Park, Ocean Beach, San Diego, Cal.

THE CHUTES. Shooting-the-Chutes at Wonderland Amusement Park in Ocean Beach was an early variation of a log ride. Flat-bottom boats guided by rails would slide down a steep ramp into a large water-filled pool. Wonderland had an extensive fun zone modeled after Coney Island's Luna Park. The Blue Streak Racer roller coaster can be seen on the left. Wonderland Park was dismantled in 1916, and several of the rides were shipped to Santa Monica's Pleasure Pier.

4405. Bird's Eye View of
Panama-California Exposition and City.
San Diego. Cal.

EXPO BIRD'S EYE. This c. 1911 aerial rendering shows the planned 1915 Panama-California Exposition grounds in Balboa Park in the foreground with downtown, the bay, Coronado, and Point Loma in the distance. A closer look reveals that the expo layout and Spanish–Colonial Revival buildings are preliminary designs that only vaguely resemble what was actually constructed. While versions of El Prado, the California Building, and Cabrillo Bridge are visible, many of the buildings, such as the Botanical Building and Spreckels Organ Pavilion, are missing. Interestingly, this configuration includes a large, never-built, man-made lake (at the left) in the canyon where the current Japanese Friendship Garden is located.

INTENSIVE FARM. One of the goals of the 1915 Panama-California Exposition was to promote San Diego's ideal climate for growing almost anything. The Intensive Farm provided a practical demonstration of what can be done on a ranch or farm in Southern California. The 14-acre farm included turkeys, chickens, bees, walnuts, avocados, and a vineyard. This exhibit was located where Spanish Village and the San Diego Zoo are today.

BALBOA PARK GREENHOUSE. Even many longtime San Diegans do not know that the famed Botanical Building was originally a T-shaped building in 1915 with a glass-covered extension on the north side. This wing had an indoor lily pond and steel trusses overhead and functioned like a greenhouse until it was demolished in 1959.

HORTON PLAZA PARK. Pictured in this 1906 postcard is Horton Plaza Park, originally referred to as simply "The Plaza." In 1870, when Alonzo Horton built his hotel, the Horton House, he developed this small plaza on the opposite side of D Street for his hotel guests and public gatherings. The early park was mostly dirt surrounded by palms. Hanging above the plaza was an arc light powerful enough to illuminate the entire block. In 1882, a drinking fountain was installed, and in 1886, the bandstand seen here was erected.

WEATHER KIOSK. In 1909, Horton Plaza Park was chosen as the site for a weather kiosk provided by the US Weather Bureau. The kiosk was designed like a miniature Greek temple and was centered in the east walkway. It was white enameled cast iron with glass panels to allow views of meteorological instruments, bulletins, and charts. An opening at the top collected and measured rainfall. In this postcard image, the landmark fountain had not yet been constructed.

$2,000,000 U. S. GRANT HOTEL AND PLAZA

GROWTH AROUND THE PARK. Not only did the palms get taller, but the buildings surrounding Horton Plaza Park grew as well. In 1905, the Horton House hotel was razed to make room for the 11-story U.S. Grant Hotel. Ulysses S. Grant Jr. (son of the former US president) built the $1.5-million hotel to honor his father. To coincide with the opening of the hotel in 1910, architect Irving Gill designed the park's dome-topped fountain.

SAN DIEGO, CAL.
New Year's Night
Mme. Tromben
singing in open air.
Temperature 52
at 9:30 P. M.

NEW YEAR'S EVE. This c. 1912 postcard commemorates New Year's Eve in Horton Plaza Park. "Mme. Tromben" appears to be referring to opera soprano Elisa Tromben. The Broadway Fountain, at the park's center, was modeled after a monument in Greece and was one of the first fountains to use underwater lighting. City electrician Harry Brown warned that "death will come to some poor unfortunate" when the lights were turned on at the 1910 dedication ceremony. But the celebration proceeded, and thankfully, no one was electrocuted.

137A:—The Beautiful Dance Casino, Mission Beach, San Diego, Calif.

BEACH CASINO. This c. 1930 postcard features the Dance Casino in Mission Beach, which was originally built as part of the Mission Beach Amusement Center by John D. Spreckels in 1925 to promote real estate and ridership on his electric railway. Many people associate the term "casino" with gambling, but during this period, "casino" referred to a dance hall. This amusement center was renamed Belmont Park in 1955.

4202. Am gaining in strength daily, on the Beach, near San Diego, Cal.

BEACH FASHION. This c. 1915 postcard shows how much beach attire has changed in 100-plus years. This strongman is wearing a knitted wool "tank suit." The women appear to be wearing Victorian-era bathing costumes that were no longer fashionable after 1910. Pale skin was still a symbol of the upper class, so very little flesh was exposed. Tans did not become fashionable until the 1930s.

132A:—Main Entrance to Bath House, Mission Beach, San Diego, Calif.

BATH PLUNGE. The Bath House at Mission Beach, c. 1925, also known as the "Natatorium" or "Plunge," was a 60-by-175-foot swimming pool. The 400,000-gallon pool was said to be the largest saltwater pool in the world in 1925, and admission was free. The building that enclosed the pool was designed by architect Frank Stevenson in the Spanish–Colonial Revival style that was popularized at the 1915 Panama-California Exposition in Balboa Park. The postcard below shows the original fountain at the far end of the pool. The saltwater became too much of a strain on the filtration system, so the pool was switched to freshwater in 1940. The Plunge could then be called the largest indoor heated pool in Southern California. The remodeled pool remains in 2023, but the building around it was replaced in 2019 and no longer has its Spanish charm.

133A:—The Natatorium, Mission Beach, San Diego, Calif.

OCEANSIDE PLUNGE. This swimming pool, with a slide and observation gallery, was completed in 1905 for "the purpose of healthful amusement." The plunge shared a building with the Oceanside Gas & Electric Light Co. plant that was located on the beach where the Junior Seau Beach Community Center is now located. Saltwater was pumped from the ocean into the 90,000-gallon pool and heated to a toasty 83 degrees. The rings hanging over the pool are known as "traveling rings." Water basketball was also a popular pool pastime. The Oceanside Plunge was torn down in 1927.

SUNSET CLIFFS PARK. Envisioned in anticipation of the 1915 Panama-California Exposition, Sunset Cliffs Park was initially developed by Albert G. Spalding, cofounder of the Spalding sporting goods company, at a cost of $2 million. It included Japanese-style gardens, cobblestone pathways, palm-thatched shelters, and rustic arched bridges. Stairways led down the cliffs, where rock formations and caves could be explored. Following Spalding's death in 1915, the park's unique features fell into disrepair and eventually disappeared.

MISSION CLIFF GARDENS. Located at the far end of Adams Avenue and Park Boulevard, overlooking the farmlands of Mission Valley, was a five-acre botanical garden created in 1890 called The Bluffs. Later renamed Mission Cliff Gardens, the San Diego Cable Railway Company developed the site as an appealing attraction to increase ridership. The park featured a large pavilion, playground, merry-go-round, and shooting gallery. Later, a Japanese garden, an aviary, and view pergolas were added. In 1942, the former park was sold and subdivided into residential lots. Scattered pieces of the park remain, including the entry gate and cobblestone walls along Adams Avenue.

OSTRICH RIDE. E.J. Johnson and his American Ostrich Company received a deed to operate an ostrich farm on A Avenue between Eighth and Ninth Streets in Coronado in 1887. The farm was operated both as a tourist attraction and an ostrich feather farm. In the early 1900s, W.H. "Harvey" Bentley took over the business, and he later moved the ostriches to Mission Cliff Gardens. Ostrich feathers were used for ladies' hats, boas, and stoles and sold for $350 a pound. Visitors particularly enjoyed the ostrich racing, where the large birds could reach a speed of up to 45 miles per hour. The rider in this postcard does not seem very enthused.

Feeding Oranges to the Ostriches
at The Ostrich Farm, San Diego, Cal.

OSTRICH FEEDING. Visitors to the Mission Cliff Gardens could admire the world's largest birds for an additional fee. One guest recalled, "I remember giving one of the birds an orange to eat. He gulped it whole and you could see the shape of the orange as it slowly sank down his neck." As an ode to the community's history, a pair of ostriches currently crowns the entrance sign to University Heights.

TENTS ON THE BEACH. Located just south of the Hotel del Coronado, Tent City was established in 1900 as a discount alternative for visitors who could not afford to stay at the hotel. A 1903 Tent City brochure notes the many comforts and conveniences, such as sewage and water systems, free ice, electric lights, a public pool, street cars, long-distance telephones, a barbershop, hairdressing parlors, laundry, and mail delivered twice a day. Tent City even had a weekly publication, *Coronado Tent City News*.

TENT CITY. This aerial view of Coronado's Tent City, looking south, was postmarked in 1908. Accessible by trolley, Tent City featured restaurants, a soda fountain, a library, a grocery store, shops, a theater, a bandstand, saltwater baths, a dance pavilion, children's rides, and its own police department. But it was the vast, sandy beaches that brought visitors to this area.

2830 Pavilion, Tent City. Coronado, California.

DANCE PAVILION. In 1910, a huge dance pavilion and boardwalk were added to Tent City. At one time, it was the largest dance hall on the Pacific Coast. The structure later became a bowling alley and skating rink. Continuing down the boardwalk, visitors could see a seal tank, an ostrich farm, and monkey cages.

Tent City Life.

TENT CITY LIFE. Tent City was a huge success. It grew from 300 tents in its first year to more than 1,000 three years later. A 1903 Tent City brochure reveals the affordability of tent living: An eight-by-ten-foot unfurnished tent without an awning was $1.50 a week. Depending on size, a furnished tent could cost from $3.50 to $6 per week. "A furnished tent comprises: Matting on boarded floor, comfortable beds, bedding, tables, wash stands, rocking chairs, folding chairs, camp chairs, lamp, clean linen, towels, water, and daily care of tent and laundry of tent linen."

3850—Children's Bathing Pool, Tent City, San Diego, California.

CHILDREN'S BATHING POOL. A large public pool at Coronado's Tent City provided an alternative for those who were tired of swimming in the ocean. It also provided an opportunity to wash off. The pool included a large slide and a shallow section for small children. Adjacent to the pool was a carousel that was moved to Balboa Park in 1922 and is still in operation today. This pool, and the rest of Tent City, closed in 1938.

Japanese Tea Garden, Coronado, San Diego, Cal.

CORONADO'S TEA GARDEN. Feeding America's fascination with Japanese culture at the turn of the century, John D. Spreckels commissioned Japanese art supplier George Turner Marsh of San Francisco to design and build a Japanese tea garden near the Hotel del Coronado and golf course. The garden was a replica of those in Tokyo and Yokohama with materials imported from Japan and San Francisco. In 1902, the gardens were open to the public for 25¢. Due to heavy storms in 1905, the garden was relocated to the Spreckels estate and eventually closed in 1936.

472. ENTRANCE, WONDERLAND PARK, BY NIGHT, OCEAN BEACH, SAN DIEGO, CAL.

SAN DIEGO'S FIRST AMUSEMENT PARK. This is a nighttime view of the entrance to Wonderland Amusement Park that is featured on the cover. Quoting from the July 3, 1913, *San Diego Union*: "With one swift move of the hand at the big switchboard at 'Wonderland' last night, Mayor Charles F. O'Neall of San Diego opened the big playground at Ocean Beach just as the clock struck seven. The blaze of light that followed was a startler to the crowds that were waiting outside the closed gates clamoring for admittance." After the park closed, the gatehouses were salvaged and converted into an apartment building on Lotus Street in Ocean Beach.

4726 BALL ROOM, WONDERLAND PARK, OCEAN BEACH, SAN DIEGO, CAL.

WONDERLAND BALL ROOM. Over 20,000 people attended opening day at Wonderland Amusement Park in Ocean Beach. Wonderland boasted 40 attractions, including the Ball Room, seen here illuminated by hundreds of festive lights. It was reported that the park utilized 22,000 tungsten lights to outline all of the buildings.

WONDERLAND BAND. The Band Stand and Casino at Wonderland are pictured around 1913. The Casino's restaurant was built over the ocean on a pier and could serve 550 patrons. Competition from the 1915 Panama-California Exposition and winter storms led to Wonderland's closure in 1916.

WELCOMING FLAMINGOS. This 1960s-era postcard shows the entrance to the San Diego Zoo as many locals remember it. After passing through the turnstiles, visitors would be greeted by a lagoon filled with dozens of pink flamingos. The zoo, founded by Dr. Harry Wegeforth, unveiled its first exhibits in Balboa Park in 1922. The initial zoo was little more than a row of small cages along Park Boulevard. Most of the animals had been on display at the 1915–1916 exposition and Wonderland Amusement Park.

Oriental beauty abounds at the Japanese Tea Garden

JAPANESE TEA GARDEN

JAPANESE TEA GARDEN. Following in the footsteps of Coronado's earlier Tea House, this pavilion and garden in Balboa Park represented Japan at the 1915 Panama-California Exposition. Located northeast of the Botanical Building, the Tea House was designed and constructed in Japan, disassembled, then shipped to the exposition, where it was erected on site. The interior of the Tea House was also authentic, and visitors could sit on bamboo mats and enjoy rice cakes and green ice cream with their tea. The Tea House and Garden continued beyond the first exposition, through the 1935–1936 California Pacific International Exposition, and even survived America's years of war with Japan. It was not until 1955 that the exhibit was demolished to accommodate the children's zoo.

Four

ON THE WATER

83:—Aquaplaning, San Diego Bay, Calif.

AQUAPLANING. This precursor to water skiing became a popular component of fun water competitions and stunt shows. An early account notes the first recorded aquaplane rider was based in Coronado Beach as early as 1900. Note that the man on the far right wears a shirt reading "Tent City Coronado." The sport continued to be a popular recreational activity in San Diego and Coronado until the 1930s.

BAY PANORAMA. This view looks northeast toward downtown San Diego from the bay in 1904. In 1869, Alonzo Horton invested $50,000 to build a wharf at the end of Fifth Avenue, making this and adjacent streets the backbone of his New Town development. San Diego's 22 square miles of natural harbor and deepwater port, together with its mild climate, helped draw many early speculators. The handwritten message on this double postcard concludes, "This is a lovely town & a fine bay for fishing rowing & sailing."

S.D. 29   MUNICIPAL WHARF, SAN DIEGO, CALIFORNIA

MUNICIPAL WHARF. San Diego's Broadway Pier was first constructed in 1913 and was the only concrete pier on the bay at that time. It served passenger vessels and was remodeled in the 1970s. This postcard features the original wharf building with an arched entry to accommodate trucks and several railroad spurs for freight trains. The current pier building was erected in 2010 and houses a busy cruise ship terminal.

50

*e a birthday this week so I think I would let
ty of good wishes for you even 'tis good wishes off.
how for fishing rowing & sailing. Goodbye from your
Cousin Bess.*

87:—San Diego Yacht Club, Coronado, Calif.

YACHT CLUB. The San Diego Yacht Club began in 1886. Its first home was a small building on stilts at the foot of Sixth Street. In 1910, the yacht club purchased *Silver Gate*, an old Coronado ferry boat, to use as its headquarters near the Coronado ferry landing. By 1923, a clubhouse building was constructed in Coronado, as seen in this postcard. The clubhouse was moved in 1934 on two barges and towed across the channel to Point Loma. In 1962, the old clubhouse was moved to the rear of the Point Loma property while a new clubhouse was constructed, which is still in use in 2023.

Ferry between Coronado and San Diego, Cal.

FERRY BOATS. Above is the Coronado Ferry Company's 118-foot *Ramona* on San Diego Bay around 1905. Built in 1903, the *Ramona* became a familiar sight to travelers on the bay. It was a steam-powered vessel with side paddle wheels and a two-cylinder engine. The *Ramona* was the first ferry to have incandescent lights instead of oil lamps. After 28 years of faithful service, the *Ramona* was retired in 1931. It was later converted into a dine-and-dance club but sadly sank at its mooring in 1937. The image below is the more-modern *San Diego*, built in 1931 for the San Diego–Coronado Ferry Company. For decades, the 191-foot *San Diego* performed its work shuttling people and cars between the mainland and Coronado. The completion of the San Diego–Coronado Bridge in 1969 put it out of business, and the *San Diego* was relocated to Washington State.

802 SAN DIEGO AND CORONADO FERRY, WITH PART OF U. S. FLEET IN REAR.

9-2063

FERRY BUILDING. The Coronado Ferryboat Terminal was located at the east end of Orange Avenue. It served ferries between San Diego and Coronado beginning in 1886. The first ferry, the *Coronado*, was 100 feet long and able to accommodate three horses and their buggies. The ferries would later provide passage for automobiles crossing the harbor. Under California law, ferry boats are banned from operating within 10 miles of a toll crossing, so the ferries ceased operation in 1969, when the San Diego–Coronado Bridge opened. However, in 1986, the construction fees were paid off on the bridge and the toll was removed, so the ferries began service again but now only transport pedestrians and bicycles.

LOG RAFT. Lumber magnate Simon Benson needed to get logs from Oregon's Columbia River to his mill in San Diego, so he designed football-shaped log rafts to be towed by tugs. Between 1906 and 1941, these acre-sized rafts made of Oregon logs fueled a construction boom in Southern California. When the rafts arrived in San Diego, the huge bundles were disassembled by crane at the Benson Lumber Company's mill and cut into lumber. Up to six million board feet of lumber was milled from each raft, enough "to build 460 average residences," reported the *San Diego Union* in 1935.

Towing in Log Raft containing 4,500,000 feet, for Saw Mills of San Diego, Cal.

TUNA FLEET. Take a stroll along downtown's waterfront, with its towering resort hotels and landscaped promenades, and it is hard to imagine that this area was once known as the "Tuna Capital of the World." San Diego became a key player in the tuna fishing industry in the 1880s, when Portuguese and Italian fishermen, based in La Playa, were catching fish from small boats. Starting in 1911, many tuna canneries were established for brands such as Van Camp Seafood, Chicken of the Sea, and Bumble Bee Seafoods. In its heyday, tuna fishing and canning was San Diego's third largest industry, behind only aerospace and the military. As late as 1980, San Diego still had over 100 operating tuna boats. The final blow to the local tuna industry came in 1990, when the major tuna canners vowed to purchase only dolphin-safe tuna, which eliminated the use of the nets that the San Diego fleet relied upon.

21. TUNA PACKING IN CALIFORNIA.

SAN DIEGO, LARGEST TUNA PACKING CENTER IN THE UNITED STATES.

54

MONSTER SHARK. This 16-foot, 3,000-pound shark was found tangled in the halibut net of Pete Zenovich while fishing near the Hotel del Coronado on November 23, 1910. The "monster" was then towed to San Diego and displayed at the San Diego Fish Company's wharf at the foot of D Street (Broadway). Dr. D.B. Van Wagenan identified the creature as a pilgrim (basking) shark, the second-largest living shark and one of three plankton-eating shark species, along with the whale shark and megamouth shark.

ISLAND EXCURSION. Early boat excursions in San Diego began around 1885 with trips from downtown to Roseville, Ballast Point, and Ocean Beach. By 1915, the Star & Crescent Boat Company, with a combined fleet of 16 ships, had scheduled sails to Fort Rosecrans, Imperial Beach, Tijuana, and the Coronado Islands off Baja, as seen in this 1917 postcard. In 2023, there are still many opportunities for people to go sightseeing, whale watching, or fishing on boats out of San Diego Bay. The Coronado Islands are a Mexican wildlife refuge, so people are not allowed to go ashore.

MISSION BAY ATTRACTION. SeaWorld (originally Sea World) was founded by four University of California, Los Angeles (UCLA) alumni whose original plan was to build an underwater restaurant. Instead, they created the aquatic theme park, which opened in 1964, occupying 22 acres on the shores of Mission Bay. Note that the landmark tower, added in 1968, does not appear in this early photograph. The marine zoological park had aquariums and a variety of shows featuring sea lions, otters, and dolphins. Shamu the killer whale did not debut until 1965. Due to the controversy surrounding the capture and treatment of endangered orcas, SeaWorld (which now covers 190 acres) ended its killer whale shows in 2017.

FLYING ON THE BAY. This 1965 postcard shows one of SeaWorld's hydrofoil boats sponsored by the Richfield Oil Company. These boats used wing-like foils to lift the hull out of the water, allowing the vessel to go faster. The hydrofoils would take 28 park visitors on a splashy loop around Mission Bay during the summer months. In the late 1980s, this unique ride was permanently retired.

Five

LOCAL HOSPITALITY

Escondido Hotel, Escondido, Cal.

ESCONDIDO HOTEL. The hospitality industry came to the town of Escondido with the construction of the 100-room Escondido Hotel in 1886. The hotel, seen in this c. 1915 postcard, stood on a knoll on the east end of Grand Avenue. Upon the construction of the Escondido Depot at the west end of Grand Avenue, the hotel inaugurated a free shuttle service to and from the depot by horse-drawn bus. Eventually, the Escondido Streetcar Company connected the depot to the hotel. Sadly, this quaint Victorian hotel was demolished in 1925.

HORTON HOUSE. An 1883 photograph shows the Horton House, a two-story hotel located on D Street (Broadway). In 1869, the *San Diego Bulletin* noted, "The great need of this town is about to be supplied by A.E. Horton, Esq., who will immediately erect, on the northwest corner of Fourth and D Streets, a palatial brick edifice, for hotel purposes. It is to contain a hundred rooms and to be fitted up with elegant furniture and all modern improvements." The hotel opened in 1870 and cost $150,000. Hotel guests paid $2.50 per day with meals. The Horton House came down in 1905 to make way for an even grander hotel, the U.S. Grant Hotel.

INTERNATIONAL–SAN MIGUEL HOTEL. When Frank Kimball brought the Santa Fe Railroad to National City, there were only four hotels in town. A fifth hotel was constructed near the new depot in anticipation of an influx of visitors. Originally known as the International Hotel, the building was completed in 1882 by the San Diego Land and Town Company at Fifth and Twenty-Second Streets. In 1906, the hotel was moved to Sixth and Twenty-Third Streets and renamed the Hotel San Miguel, as seen in this postcard.

LAKESIDE INN
LAKESIDE, CALIFORNIA

Golf, Auto Racing, Mineral Water, Fishing and Hunting

LAKESIDE INN. Completed in 1887, the Lakeside Inn was built during the height of the Great Boom. The four-story inn was located near Lindo Lake and included 80 spacious rooms. The Gothic-Victorian design was similar to the Hotel del Coronado, so the inn got the nickname "the Coronado of the Hills." Rates at the inn were $2 per day. Around 1900, Fr. Henry Eummelan assumed management of the inn and established the Kneipp Sanitarium at the hotel. In 1904, the inn was purchased by John H. Gay, who built an auto racetrack adjacent to the hotel. By 1920, the inn could no longer stay in business and was demolished.

KENILWORTH INN
RAMONA, CALIF.

KENILWORTH INN. Destroyed by fire in 1943, the Kenilworth Hotel opened in 1887 at Sixth and Main Streets as the Ramona Hotel. It was built by Milton Santee, who was responsible for renaming the town from Nuevo to Ramona in an attempt to capitalize on the famed Helen Hunt Jackson's novel of the same name. The hotel's name was later changed to the Ricker Hotel before its new owner, Ida May Roques Kearney, dubbed it the Kenilworth Inn.

Ball Room, Hotel del Coronado. Coronado, California.

BEAUTIFUL BALLROOM. The 1888 Hotel del Coronado is still very much around, but its most dramatic space, the ballroom, no longer resembles this early postcard image. Note the Moorish lanterns on the railing, the perimeter catwalk, and abundant daylight from the high windows. In 1961, the ballroom was "re-muddled," and painted drywall now entombs the beautiful woodwork and blocks the upper windows, while acoustic panels conceal the catwalk and exposed wood ceiling. In 2023, the current owners are taking steps to potentially restore the ballroom.

Palm Court, Hotel del Coronado. Coronado, California.

SUMMERHOUSE AT THE DEL. The large tropical courtyard (or garden patio) at the center of the Hotel del Coronado originally contained a fountain with a seminude bronze female figure known as the "Naiad Queen." A local newspaper reporter in 1888 thought she should be named "Miss Few Clothes." Complaints from guests eventually led to the fountain being removed in 1909. In 1912, a rustic summerhouse was built where the fountain once stood. It can be seen in this c. 1915 postcard. The small pavilion was used for teas, luncheons, and weddings and appeared in the 1919 silent film *The Married Virgin* starring Rudolph Valentino.

HOTEL BREWSTER. SAN DIEGO. CALIFORNIA.

HOTEL BREWSTER. This hotel was located at the southeast corner of Fourth Avenue and C Street. Completed in 1887 (one year before the Hotel del Coronado), the 150-room Victorian-era hotel was developed and owned by Horace Brewster, who spent the extravagant sum of $150,000 to create his dream hotel. According to *The Golden Era* magazine, it contained a ballroom, shops, elevators, "exquisitely frescoed" interiors, live music during the lunch and dinner hours from "one of the best string quartettes," and meals prepared by the "best class of French cooks that can be had." The Hotel Brewster was torn down in 1934. In 2023, the site houses a pizza shop.

Hotel Robinson, San Diego, Cal.

HOTEL ROBINSON. Originally known as the Florence Hotel, this large building was located at the corner of Fourth and Fir Streets starting in 1884. It was considered a premier luxury resort and offered commanding views of the city, bay, and ocean. The hotel included 200 steam-heated rooms, 70 baths, large porches, a sun parlor, a ballroom, a restaurant, and a landscaped exterior courtyard. It was renamed the Hotel Robinson in about 1904 by owner Charles W. Robinson. Architect William Sterling Hebbard is said to have designed the added third story and front porch. The 1906 postcard below shows an extensive and ornate dining room with fluted columns and frescoed ceilings. The hotel changed its name again to Casa Loma but was razed in the 1940s.

Dining Room Hotel Robinson, San Diego, Cal.

CALIFORNIA HOTEL. The Eagles had their Hotel California, and San Diego had one too. The hotel was initially named the less-catchy Selwyn & Allison Block when it opened on Fifth Avenue in 1887. The commercial storefront included a butcher shop owned by George A. Selwyn and James M. Allison. By the late 1880s, Selwyn & Allison had expanded to three locations, including one in National City. In 1903, the upper rooms were renovated for the newly established Santa Rosa Hotel. By 1926, the building was renamed once again, and the front desk could have greeted guests by saying "Welcome to the Hotel California."

CALIFORNIA HOTEL

MAX F. A. SHIEVE, PROP.

"MAKE OUR HOTEL YOUR HOME"

PHONE MAIN 6551

553 FIFTH AVENUE
SAN DIEGO. CALIF.

1178 – HOTEL BALBOA, PACIFIC BEACH, SAN DIEGO, CALIFORNIA.

HOTEL BALBOA. Completed in 1888 for the San Diego College of Letters campus, north of what is now Garnet Avenue, the building was designed by James W. Reid, architect of the Hotel del Coronado. It was one of the first major structures in Pacific Beach and was surrounded by lemon groves with views of the ocean and distant mountains. The college closed in 1891, and the building became Hotel Balboa in 1904. In 1910, it was leased for use as the San Diego Army and Navy Academy, calling itself the "West Point of the West." The Brown Military Academy took over the site in 1937. The building was eventually demolished in 1958 for a shopping mall.

4177. U. S. Grant Hotel, showing Tents on Roof Garden and Wireless Equipment, San Diego, Cal.

Palm Court, U. S. Grant Hotel, San Diego, Cal.

ROOFTOP TENTS. The Hotel del Coronado has its Tent City, but the U.S. Grant Hotel had its "Tent Roof" to accommodate overflowing crowds for the nearby exposition. Described on the back of this 1915 postcard, "U.S. Grant Hotel, San Diego, Cal. showing the unique manner in which the congestion of the hotel was relieved. Twenty-two tents on one of the roof gardens and each one completely furnished as a sleeping apartment. These tents are preferred by 'air-cranks' to the more luxurious rooms of the hotel of which there are 500."

PALM COURT. After five years of construction and $1.9 million expended, the U.S. Grant Hotel opened its doors on October 15, 1910. This c. 1915 view looks south from the hotel across Broadway toward Horton Plaza Park. In the mid-1950s, during a tourism boom, the Grant underwent a major renovation, and this lovely second-floor Palm Court was enclosed to become the Palm Ballroom. The fountain was removed and sent to the Agua Caliente Racetrack.

SALT WATER PLUNGE. As part of the original design, the U.S. Grant Hotel included two large saltwater swimming pools fed by water piped up D Street (Broadway) from San Diego Bay. This 1912 postcard shows one of the pools, which was located in the basement below the sidewalk. The grid at the ceiling is made up of glass pavers set in the concrete sidewalk to bring daylight into the basement.

BIVOUAC GRILL. This c. 1915 postcard shows the cavern-like Bivouac Grill, a popular dining spot for guests of the U.S. Grant Hotel. Note the absence of windows because the restaurant was in the basement. The U.S. Grant was slated for demolition in 1979, but Christopher Sickels purchased the hotel and spared it from the wrecking ball. Later in 1979, the U.S. Grant Hotel was added to the National Register of Historic Places.

Stratford Inn. Del Mar, San Diego County, Cal.

STRATFORD INN. Built on 10 acres overlooking the beach in Del Mar, the South Coast Land Company constructed the grand resort hotel seen here in 1922. Prominent Los Angeles architect John C. Austin designed the hotel in the English Tudor style, with steeply pitched roofs and exposed timbers on the facades. The hotel was modeled after the Elizabethan buildings in Stratford-on-Avon in England. The Stratford Inn officially opened on March 9, 1909, and later became a hot spot for Hollywood elites who were in town to watch the nearby horse races. The Stratford underwent a $250,000 renovation in 1925 and was renamed Hotel Del Mar a year later. The 1911 postcard below shows the large lobby and a handwritten "X" at the front desk. The message on the back from Clara reads, "This is where I work." The hotel eventually closed in 1963 and was demolished in 1969. Since 1989, L'Auberge Del Mar hotel has occupied the site. The Stratford's legacy is strong because Del Mar's unofficial style remains English Tudor.

Lobby at "Stratford Inn", Del Mar, Cal.

FREE SAMPLE ROOMS FOR
COMMERCIAL MEN ON GROUND FLOOR
FREE BUS TO AND FROM TRAINS AND BOATS
HOTEL RICHMOND
COR. SECOND AND F STS., SAN DIEGO, CAL.
RATES, 50c TO $2.00 PER DAY
A. M. CROW, PROPRIETOR

INTERIOR VIEWS

HOTEL RICHMOND. This 1909 postcard shows both interior and exterior views of the Hotel Richmond. The 1888 Victorian hotel was located at the corner of Second and F Streets in downtown San Diego. An ad from 1910 refers to the Richmond as "strictly first-class." As early as 1915, the hotel became a Black-owned business and was one of the early residential hotels to welcome African American guests. In 1950, the hotel's name was changed to the Tower Hotel, and it was one of many older buildings demolished in the early 1980s to make way for Horton Plaza mall.

Absolutely Fireproof.
Rates $1.00 and up.

Tioga Hotel, Cor. 3rd and B Sts., San Diego, Cal.

TIOGA HOTEL. Located at the corner of Third and B Streets in downtown San Diego, the 50-room "absolutely fireproof" Tioga Hotel was designed by noted architects the Quayle Brothers in 1918. Charles and Edward Quayle would also design Balboa Stadium and the old police headquarters, now a shopping and dining spot on West Harbor Drive. Starting in 1946, the Tioga became a US Veterans Administration (VA) building that housed the first VA outpatient health care available for San Diego and Imperial Valley veterans.

POPPIES AND PIGEONS. The Maryland Hotel, at Sixth and F Streets, was constructed in 1913 and is currently known as the Andaz Hotel. The 300-room hostelry began as the Sefton Hotel, built by influential banker Joseph W. Sefton Jr. It was designed by famed architect William Hebbard and is the only surviving hotel from his portfolio. The hotel was renamed the Maryland Hotel in 1916. The postcards featured here show two charming aspects of the Maryland that have been lost. The hotel once had a cheerful, orange-hued dining area called the Poppy Room (above) that celebrated California's state flower. Up on the roof, the Maryland Hotel had a large garden with views of the "sunshine seaport" (below). The roof contained pigeon coops that housed Victoria crown pigeons, admired for their elegant blue peacock-like crests.

CALIFORNIA CARLSBAD HOTEL AND DINING ROOM

CARLSBAD MINERAL SPRINGS HOTEL. In 1882, mineral springs were discovered in Carlsbad, which spurred the development of the city. An 85-room hotel and spa called the Carlsbad Hotel was the city's first hotel in 1887 and tapped into the mineral springs. Tourists and health-seekers flocked to the hotel before it was lost in a fire in 1896. In 1930, a luxurious new Spanish Revival–style hotel opened called the California-Carlsbad Mineral Springs Hotel & Spa, seen in the image above. The hotel welcomed such notables as Greta Garbo, Bing Crosby, and John Wayne. Despite its early success, the hotel suffered through years of financial trouble and was converted into a retirement home in 1957. The large garden patio featured the famous "Weeping Eucalyptus Tree" (below), which the hotel was built around. The legend goes that many years ago, a Spanish señorita would sit below the tree waiting for her sea captain to return. When his ship was lost, she died of a broken heart, and the tree's limbs bowed and its leaves fell like tears as if mourning the tragic couple. Years later, the Weeping Eucalyptus Tree apparently fell victim to disease and was cut down. The hotel was demolished in 1996, but the entry tower and front facade were rebuilt to resemble the 1930 design.

CARLSBAD HOTEL and MINERAL SPRINGS — CARLSBAD-BY-THE-SEA, CALIFORNIA

Patio View, Showing Famous Weeping Eucalyptus Tree   08-H2410

CASA DE PICO. This charming, faux adobe Spanish casa with a large, landscaped patio was built as a unique motor hotel in 1940. Skilled architect Richard Requa cleverly tucked all the parking in garages at the perimeter, keeping vehicles out of view. Some sharp-eyed locals may recognize this building as the original home of Bazaar Del Mundo. The motor hotel was converted into colorful shops and restaurants in 1971 by Diane Powers. Since 2009, the complex has been known as Fiesta de Reyes and is part of the Old Town San Diego State Historic Park, established in 1969.

COZY INN. Another local motel/auto court was the Cozy Inn, located at 5018 El Cajon Boulevard, seen in this c. 1930 postcard. The advent of the automobile enabled travelers to freely explore the country in ways they never could before. A 1927 *New York Times* article stated that "touring motorists can now sleep in bungalows, if they do not want to pitch tents." Campgrounds and lodges with rows of small cabins or shacks began to pop up along popular highways, providing weary travelers with a place to sleep. The Cozy Inn Auto Court even had its own gas pumps and grocery store.

Hotel El San Luis, Rey-by-the-Sea, Ocean Side, Cal.

BEACH HOTEL. This Arts & Crafts–style beach resort opened in Oceanside in 1904 and was originally named El San Luis Rey Hotel in honor of the nearby Spanish mission. Andrew Jackson Myers, the city's founder, began marketing the town as a seaside resort as early as 1883. The hotel was located on Third (now Pier View Way) and Pacific Streets, just north of the pier. The hotel was frequented by pioneering film director Cecil B. DeMille, who filmed his silent movie *The Rose of Rancho* in Oceanside in 1914. The Beach Hotel was torn down in 1966.

SAN DIEGO'S finest POLYNESIAN RESTAURANT

TIKI TRAGEDY. The Hanalei Hotel was one of Mission Valley's oldest hotels, built in 1959, and was originally a 66-unit motor hotel known as Rancho Presidio. Seven years later, hotelier Charles Brown invested $3.5 million to remodel and enlarge the hotel, adopting the Polynesian tiki style to satisfy America's post–World War II fascination with the South Pacific. The hotel included the Islands restaurant with elaborate tiki décor and tropical drinks. In a heartbreaking move, the hotel's island charm and iconic sign were obliterated by a 2006 remodel. The now faceless hotel is currently known as Crowne Plaza Mission Valley.

LANIER HOTEL,
THIRD AND ASH STS., SAN DIEGO, CALIFORNIA

LANIER HOTEL. This hotel was located on Third Avenue and Ash Street and was designed by famed architects William Hebbard and Irving Gill. Hebbard completed the hotel in about 1908 after his partnership with Gill had ended. The building's design clearly showcases Irving Gill's developing style with its simple stucco facades, flat roof, and dramatic arches. A 1915 ad noted that the hotel was only a 10-minute ride from the Panama-California Exposition in Balboa Park. The Lanier Hotel promoted its large Sun Parlor (below), calling it a "spacious court, and beautiful garden filled with flowers, ferns, rare palms, and other tropical plants adding a delightful home-like air which makes this quiet place of sojourn unusually attractive to the family." The date of the hotel's demolition is unknown.

SUN PARLOR OF THE LANIER HOTEL, THIRD AND ASH STREETS, SAN DIEGO, CALIF.   J. W. GANZHORN, MGR.

Up here seeing all San Diego from the El Cortez Sky Room

Acclaimed by artists and globe trotters to be one of the world's great inspirational, panoramic views ... by bonvivants for its excellence of luncheons, libations and service.

"Drinking in the Sky"

SAN DIEGO, CALIFORNIA

EL CORTEZ HOTEL. One of San Diego's most recognized buildings is the El Cortez, although its look has changed over the years. Richard Robinson Jr. financed the construction of the El Cortez, a Spanish Colonial Revival hotel, which opened in 1927 as the tallest building in San Diego. Ten years later, a large "El Cortez" rooftop sign was installed, which could be seen for miles. In 1940, the Sky Room bar was added to the top floor with a 360-degree view of downtown. In 1956, the hotel underwent a remodel, which included the addition of the world's second outdoor hydroelectric-ram glass elevator (below). The elevator was installed on the outside face of the El Cortez and gave passengers a thrilling ride with breathtaking views of the city and bay. In 1978, the building was sold to evangelist Morris Cerullo and became a school of evangelism. By the late 1990s, after several more sales, the El Cortez had become rundown and was threatened with demolition. In 2000, the building was restored to its 1927 appearance, without the glass elevator and Sky Room, and it eventually became condominiums.

EL CORTEZ NEON. This c. 1960 nighttime postcard shows off the dramatic neon lighting that was added in conjunction with the 1956 remodel. The new glass elevator was nicknamed the "Starlight Express." Red, blue, pink, green, and gold stars climb up the elevator shaft and surround the "Sky Room" letters. While it is often preferred to restore a building back to its original appearance, sometimes later changes become historical themselves and worthy of preservation. Sadly, this colorful aspect of the El Cortez Hotel's history has been lost.

Six

AIR CAPITAL
OF THE WEST

AIR CADETS. This postcard of pilot trainees in San Diego was postmarked December 27, 1941, just 20 days after the Japanese attack on Pearl Harbor. The two-seat training planes are PT-22 Recruits, designed and built by Ryan Aeronautical Company, headquartered in San Diego. A 1935 postcard folder sums up San Diego's strong links to aviation, stating, "The city has been the scene of much aviation activity since 1910. Both army and navy have important aviation fields here, and Lindbergh's plane was built here. The city's new municipal airport, one of the best in America, has been named for the famous flier who started at San Diego."

V FOR VICTORY. In 1922, former Army Air Corps pilot T. Claude Ryan came to San Diego and began a flying school and aerial sightseeing company. He later went on to establish Ryan Airlines, Ryan Aeronautical Company, and Ryan School of Aeronautics at Lindbergh Field in 1927. In 1925, Ryan Airlines became the first commercial airline to operate out of San Diego. After the United States entered World War II, there was a high demand for training planes, and the Ryan PT-22 was ordered in large numbers. This postcard shows a group of PT-22s readying pilots for the war. These Ryan training planes remain popular aircraft for museums and collectors.

SEAPLANE CENTRAL. San Diego, and Coronado's North Island in particular, became instrumental in the design and flight testing of seaplanes. North Island was ideal because a natural channel, known as the Spanish Bight, created a shallow bay, perfect for a seaplane runway. In 1911, Glenn Curtiss created the first successful seaplane in the United States, flying from North Island in his "hydroaeroplane" to the cruiser USS *Pennsylvania*. This postcard features a Glenn Martin Model S floatplane in San Diego Bay around 1915.

AVIATION MEET. Wealthy New York businessman Harry Harkness formed the Aero Club of San Diego in 1910 and sponsored an aviation exhibition at the Coronado Country Club's polo grounds. The grandstand faced North Island with views to Point Loma. One of the world's premier aviators, Glenn Curtiss, participated in the event, which took place in January 1911. Curtiss and his aviators dazzled the audience of 10,000 with a series of heart-stopping aerial stunts and groundbreaking records.

FLIGHT
BY
ROCKWELL
FIELD
AVIATORS
OVER
SAN DIEGO
CELEBRATING
PEACE
NOV. 27, 1918
19©18
PHOTOGRAPHED
BY
W.E. AVERRETT

CELEBRATING PEACE. On November 27, 1918, San Diegans witnessed the sight of approximately 200 Army and Navy biplanes flying over downtown to celebrate the end of World War I. Many came from Rockwell Field, which was located on Coronado's North Island and was the home of the first military airplane training school, the US Army Signal Corps Aviation School, established in 1912. While it was an impressive sight, this image was actually made up of several combined photographs.

94:—Army Planes Refueling in the air over San Diego, Calif.

AERIAL REFUELING. To address the fuel limitation problems in early airplanes, the fliers at Rockwell Field in San Diego developed a system for mid-air refueling. The first successful aerial refueling took place on June 27, 1923, when a de Havilland DH-4B bomber passed gasoline through a hose to another DH-4B flying beneath it. This dramatic postcard was mailed in 1924 and appears to show that famous flight above the San Diego coast.

741 "WINGS OVER SAN DIEGO". SHOWING NEW CIVIC CENTER BUILDING.

SAN DIEGO. CALIFORNIA   46382

WINGS OVER SAN DIEGO. Promotional postcards such as this showcased San Diego's new Civic Center Building on the waterfront. The building was constructed utilizing Works Progress Administration grant funds. Pres. Franklin D. Roosevelt officially dedicated the building on July 16, 1938, although the building did not open for another five months. Even in the days before digital editing, postcard photographs were often colorized and manipulated. These three planes, probably Ryan Aeronautical Company trainers, appear to be composited in for dramatic effect.

SPIRIT OF ST. LOUIS. A 1927 headline in the *San Diego Union* read, "Lindbergh Winging His Way from San Diego to Paris." Here, Capt. Charles A. Lindbergh (the tall one) is seen just before his departure from North Island's Rockwell Field on May 10, 1927. He is standing next to his San Diego–built plane, the *Spirit of St. Louis*, with plans to land in St. Louis before heading to New York and finally Paris. Lindbergh completed the world's first nonstop transatlantic solo flight on May 21, 1927, in 33 hours, 30 minutes.

NEW AIRPORT. In 1928, San Diego Municipal Airport–Lindbergh Field was the first federally certified airfield to serve all aircraft types, including seaplanes. Charles Lindbergh agreed to lend his name to the airport, located near the site of the Ryan Airlines factory, and it soon became a hub for US military and general aviation operations. By the 1930s, cargo and airmail services were established on-site. Round airfields were rare and inefficient, so the artist's rendering in this c. 1927 postcard apparently does not accurately show how Lindbergh Field was configured when it opened.

724:—LINDBERGH FIELD AND ADMINISTRATION BUILDING. SAN DIEGO. CALIFORNIA.

© Herz

LINDBERGH FIELD. On August 16–18, 1928, the San Diego Chamber of Commerce hosted the Western Aviation Progress Exhibition to commemorate the dedication of Lindbergh Field and the 25th anniversary of the Wright brothers' first powered flight. The exhibition included a parade down Broadway, parachute jumps, and a mass flight over San Diego with 400 planes from the Army, Navy, and Marine Corps. The original San Diego Municipal Airport terminal, seen above, was a small building with a red tile roof and detached waiting areas. After Pacific Southwest Airlines (PSA) established its headquarters in San Diego, it inaugurated Lindbergh Field's commercial services in 1949. The postcard below shows a later, Mid-Century Modern–style municipal airport terminal in about 1950. Commercial use continued to grow in the 1950s, and Lindbergh Field attracted regular services from other airlines like United and American. Passenger traffic expanded in the 1960s, with the new East Terminal (Terminal 1) opening in 1967. Terminal 2 opened in 1979 and was expanded in 1998. In 2023, San Diego International Airport covers 663 acres and is the busiest single-runway airport in the world.

GREETINGS FROM
U.S. NAVAL AIR Station
SAN DIEGO, California

90

NORTH ISLAND. The northern end of Coronado, known as North Island, started as a joint Army and Navy aviation station for the training of pilots. World War I gave impetus to establish US Naval Air Station San Diego, which began operations in 1917. "Air crowding" was often a complaint from both the Army and Navy, with 130 airplanes on North Island at one point making flying and landing difficult and dangerous. The c. 1920 postcard below shows a row of two-seat bombers on the flight line. In 1935, the Army departed, and Rockwell Field was transferred to the Navy. The naval air station was granted official recognition as the "Birthplace of Naval Aviation" by the House Armed Services Committee in 1963. In more recent years, the 2022 blockbuster *Top Gun: Maverick* was filmed in part at North Island Naval Air Station.

U.S. ARMY
AVIATION SCHOOL
No. 38

NORTH ISLAND
SAN DIEGO

USS SHENANDOAH. Longer than two football fields, the USS *Shenandoah* was the first rigid airship built in the United States and the first in the world to be inflated with helium. Seen here at North Island Naval Air Station in 1924, the *Shenandoah* had traveled from Lakehurst, New Jersey, and then on to Washington State. This was the first flight of a rigid airship across North America. As noted in the postcard's handwritten caption, the *Shenandoah* "blew apart" in 1925 in a severe storm over Ohio, killing 14 of the 43 persons on board.

LIBERATORS. Consolidated Aircraft Corp. (later Convair) became one of the largest civilian employers in San Diego. By 1943, approximately 40,000 were employed locally under Consolidated Vultee, of which 40 percent were women. Per a 1944 promotional booklet, "Feminine workers vary in age from youthful school-age employees who turn out bomber parts and at the same time receive high school credit for their work, to 70-year-old grandmothers who have taken their places on assembly lines until victory is won." This 1944 postcard shows the assembly line for B-24 Liberators, a key bomber during World War II.

CONSOLIDATED AIRCRAFT. Located adjacent to Lindbergh Field, Consolidated Aircraft was founded in 1923 by Maj. Reuben H. Fleet. The company moved its headquarters from Buffalo, New York, to San Diego in 1935 due to more favorable weather and proximity to North Island Naval Air Station. The back of one postcard reads, "Consolidated Aircraft Corporation Plant is the largest integral aircraft factory in the United States, where the famous PBY (Catalina) flying boats and the B-24 (*Liberator*) four-engine bombers, are constructed." Consolidated Vultee later became Convair. In 1953, Convair was purchased by General Dynamics.

FLYING BOAT. This giant seaplane is a PB2Y patrol bomber, named the Coronado, designed by Consolidated Aircraft. The US Navy invested heavily in flying boats because of their ability to take off and land without needing runways. In June 1942, Catalina PBY seaplanes sighted two Japanese aircraft carriers and their escort ships heading to attack Midway Atoll. This critical reconnaissance helped the United States gain the upper hand at the Battle of Midway, a major turning point of the war in the Pacific.

Seven

WHEN WE HAD FUN

HULA CLASS. Mainlanders enjoy a hula class at the Bali Hai restaurant in Shelter Island. San Diego's tiki craze of the 1950s–1960s was born from Americans' fascination with the South Pacific and encompassed Polynesian pop influence in its architecture, interior design, entertainment, music, food, and clothing. Although tiki's modern roots reach back before World War II, its zenith occurred around the time that Hawaii became the 50th state in 1959. The Bali Hai, originally named Christian's Hut, was constructed in 1953–1955 and was rechristened as Bali Hai, inspired by James Michener's 1947 *Tales of the South Pacific*.

713:—DEL MAR TURF CLUB, BING CROSBY, PRES., DEL MAR, NEAR SAN DIEGO, CALIFORNIA.

"WHERE THE SURF MEETS THE TURF."   42388

SURF AND TURF. In the early 1930s, a 184-acre site in the San Dieguito Valley was developed as a fairground utilizing Works Progress Administration (WPA) funds. Architects Herbert Jackson and Sam Hamill designed the fairground's Spanish Colonial Revival buildings, and the inaugural fair opened in 1936. That same year, legendary singer Bing Crosby, who was living in neighboring Rancho Santa Fe, was approached to help create a horse racing track at the fairgrounds. The Del Mar Turf Club was soon formed, and a large grandstand was constructed adjacent to a one-mile oval track, as seen in these c. 1940 postcards. Opening day in 1937 was a star-studded event with many Hollywood elites in attendance. In 1938, the track hosted a much-publicized match race between two famous horses, Seabiscuit and Ligaroti, which helped put Del Mar on the map. The race was close with Seabiscuit winning by a length. The original racetrack buildings were replaced, and summer racing season still brings big crowds to Del Mar.

GRAND STAND
DEL MAR TURF CLUB
DEL MAR, CALIF.

SKATELAND. Touted as "San Diego's Largest and Finest Roller Skating Rink," Skateland was located at Front and G Streets downtown. Skateland opened in 1947 and was constructed in the midst of the "golden age" of roller skating: the 1930s through the 1950s. The Mid-Century Modern building was trimmed with pink and blue neon and held skating classes with "all phases of skating taught." The Meridian condo tower has occupied this site since 1986.

GLACIER GARDENS. This postcard (which doubled as a decal) shows the Streamline Moderne–style ice rink, located at the intersection of Eighth Avenue and Harbor Drive, that opened on June 6, 1939. "The Gardens" were home to the San Diego Skyhawks of the Pacific Coast Hockey League and the San Diego Figure Skating Club. Later called the San Diego Arena, the 5,000-seat venue hosted four concerts from budding star Elvis Presley in 1956. Tickets were $1.50 at the door. Glacier Gardens was torn down in the mid-1960s.

DECALCOMANIA TRANSFER PICTURE

GLACIER GARDEN SAN DIEGO

To decal cut on dotted line, place in warm water and slide off to any surface. Patent 2,319,293 Other patents pending.

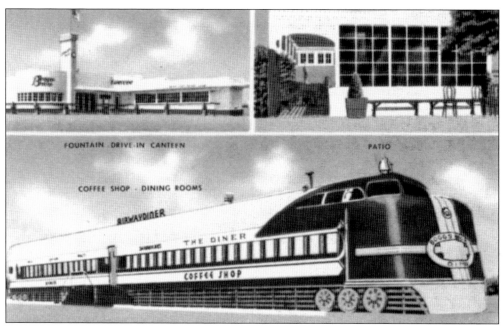

LOCOMOTIVE DINER. The Boggs Bros. Airway Diner, Canteen, and Drive-In was located at Pacific Highway and Laurel Street near Lindbergh Field and opened in 1935. Herb and Ray Boggs owned several restaurants in San Diego. This postcard, postmarked in 1949, states that "the 'Diner' is part of an actual train that operated between San Diego and Old Mexico years ago." Apparently, two railroad cars were combined with a Santa Fe streamline locomotive at one end. In 1951, this unique diner was replaced by Anthony's Fish Grotto.

RIVERBOAT RESTAURANT. The Reuben E. Lee Riverboat Restaurant was never an actual riverboat, nor was it ever on a river. It was a faux Mississippi paddle-wheeler built on a floating barge in 1969 to serve as a restaurant at the east end of Harbor Island. The popular restaurant closed in 2004 due to maintenance issues and was eventually towed to a local shipyard. In 2012, the Reuben E. Lee sank to the bottom of San Diego Bay near the Coronado Bridge.

ZORO GARDENS. The most unique and controversial exhibit at the 1935 California Pacific International Exposition in Balboa Park was the Zoro Gardens nudist colony (misspelled "Zorro" above). This postcard (strategically blurred for this book) shows 10 of the colonists posing with bows and arrows, a parrot, and not much else. These topless women and bearded men in loincloths pretended to live in a stone-lined grotto and performed daily pseudoreligious rituals to the Sun God. The Zoro Gardens program reads, "Healthy young men and women, indulging in the freedom of outdoor living in which they so devoutly believe, have opened their colony to the friendly, curious gaze of the public." Zoro Gardens survived multiple protests and went on to become the exposition's most lucrative outdoor attraction. The garden, still in a canyon between Casa de Balboa and the Fleet Science Center, is now a family-friendly butterfly garden.

BIRTH OF THE PADRES. Seen at the center-left of this 1947 aerial view is Lane Field, a minor-league baseball stadium located at the end of West Broadway at the waterfront. The ballpark was the home field of the Pacific Coast League (PCL) San Diego Padres from 1936 through 1957. The park was named after team owner Bill "Hardpan" Lane, who moved the former Hollywood Stars team to San Diego to become the Padres. In 1937, attendance grew after their PCL pennant-winning season and because of the development of their young star Ted Williams. Lane Field was vacated by the Padres following the 1957 season when they moved to Westgate Park in Mission Valley.

BULL FIGHT ARENA. Located at Third Street and Avenida Revolución in Tijuana, Mexico, the original bull ring on this site was a wood structure with seating for 2,000 spectators. It was constructed in 1904 and burned down in 1911. It was replaced in 1938 by the slightly larger bull ring seen here called Plaza El Toreo de Tijuana. Plaza El Toreo became the center of Tijuana's entertainment scene in the 1920s and 1930s, but the ring fell victim to another fire in 1957. The Plaza El Toreo was rebuilt using steel and lasted until 2007, when it was demolished. At the height of its popularity, Tijuana hosted up to 18 bullfights a year, with most attendees coming from across the border.

WORLD-CLASS STADIUM. San Diego Stadium debuted in 1967 and was renamed Jack Murphy Stadium and later Qualcomm Stadium. The $27.8-million structure was designed by Frank L. Hope and Associates, who won a National Honor Award from the American Institute of Architects (AIA) for their exemplary design, the only stadium to receive such an honor. This postcard shows the stadium before the east end was enclosed in 1997. The multipurpose stadium remains the only venue to host the Super Bowl and World Series in the same year. Despite the stadium's design pedigree and landmark eligibility, San Diego State University proceeded with demolition in 2020, constructing the much smaller Snapdragon Stadium in 2022.

GARRICK THEATRE. This modest theater at Sixth and B Streets opened on October 18, 1907, and was financed by Col. D.C. Collier. The Garrick was designed by Henry Lord Gay of San Francisco, who would later design the Western Metal Supply Co. building, now part of Petco Park. The theater was praised for its fine acoustics and good sight lines. In 1911, the name was changed to the Empress Theatre, and in 1920, it became the Strand Theatre. The theater later became a movie house and was demolished in 1923.

ANTHONY'S. Founded by Catherine "Mama" Ghio in 1946, the original Anthony's Fish Grotto was a tiny 16-seat diner at Harbor Drive and Pacific Highway. The restaurant was named after Ghio's father. At the time of its opening, Anthony's was the only commercial kitchen in San Diego that exclusively served seafood. In 1951, the restaurant moved to a larger location at Laurel Street, as seen in this postcard. In 1965, Anthony's moved to its popular Embarcadero location, where it remained until 2017. The company expanded to other locations, but Anthony's last remaining restaurant is in La Mesa.

TOP'S DINE & DANCE. This Streamline Moderne–style restaurant opened in the 1940s as Top's Nightclub at Pacific Highway and Hawthorn Street. The venue hosted renowned artists such as Nat King Cole, Shelly Winters, and Nelson Eddy. After Top's was sold, it sat vacant until the 1970s, when Tom Fat redeveloped the building and split it into two restaurants, Fat City and China Camp, and decorated the exterior with colorful neon. In 2016, a new six-story hotel was built on the site that incorporates a facsimile of the front facade and tower of the old nightclub.

TOWER BOWL, SAN DIEGO
A Bowler's Paradise, Kapa Shell Adjoining.

TOWER BOWL. This bowling alley became a recognizable Googie-style landmark when it opened at 628 West Broadway in 1941. Designed by S. Charles Lee, this "bowler's paradise" featured 28 lanes and offered a variety of food and drinks. Entertainers worked the cocktail lounge, and a meeting room provided space for social events. The impressive 80-foot-tall tower, with neon-illuminated bowling balls, was an attention-grabber until the mid-1980s, bringing in top bowlers as well as military personnel seeking wholesome entertainment. The high-rise office building One America Plaza and its trolley station replaced Tower Bowl in 1991.

CLUB HOUSE AND GRAND STAND, AGUA CALIENTE JOCKEY CLUB, TIJUANA, MEXICO   33

AGUA CALIENTE. Just across the border in Tijuana, Mexico, the Agua Caliente horse racing track (above) drew 20,000 spectators, mostly from California, on opening day in 1929. The 1930 postcard below shows the ornate, palace-like interior of the Casino and Gold Bar at Hotel Agua Caliente. The message written on the postcard reads, "Jake, won a couple or three dollars at this table." The casino-hotel-resort covered 655 acres and cost about $10 million to build. An *LA Times* reporter wrote in 1929 that "there isn't another place on the continent, outside of a U.S. Mint, where you can see so much money piled up before your eyes at one time. Its only rival in the world is Monte Carlo." In 1934, the head of the Fox Film Corporation "discovered" 16-year-old Rita Hayworth dancing at the Caliente Club and quickly arranged for a screen test. The legalization of casino gambling in Nevada in 1931 and the repeal of Prohibition in 1933 drastically reduced attendance at Agua Caliente, and the resort closed in 1935. In 2023, Agua Caliente is known as Caliente Hipódromo, with a casino, concert venue, and greyhound racing.

X.50   ELABORATE INTERIOR OF CASINO AND FAMOUS GOLD BAR, HOTEL AGUA CALIENTE, TIJUANA, MEXICO

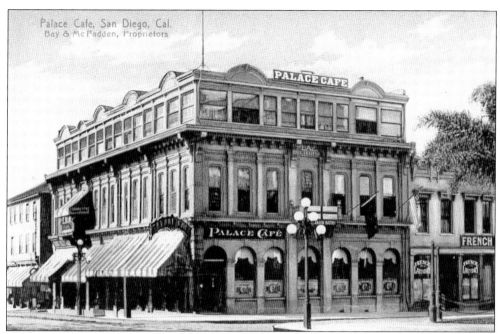

PALACE CAFÉ. This c. 1910 postcard image might look like Paris, France, but it is actually the corner of Fourth and Plaza Streets in downtown San Diego. Not much is known about the Palace Café, but the back of the postcard below calls it "the Handsomest, High Class Café in the West." One can see in the postcard above that the café was on the ground floor of the three-story Plaza Building, which faced Horton Plaza Park (note the palm fronds on the right). The Cabrillo Theater replaced the French Laundry next door in 1915. The second-floor tenant of the Plaza Building would later be dentist E.R. Parker, who billed himself as "Painless Parker." The interior of the Palace Café was festooned with Baroque ornamentation, frescoed ceiling murals, mosaic tile floors, and six-globe chandeliers. The Plaza Building was demolished in 1982 to make way for Horton Plaza mall.

THE ISTHMUS. Like the current San Diego County Fair in Del Mar, the 1915 Panama-California Exposition in Balboa Park had many large exhibition halls dedicated to education and product displays, but it also had a fun zone filled with oddities and rides. Named the Isthmus, after the Isthmus of Panama, the north end of the exposition grounds contained, according to the 1915 guidebook, "the best array of entertainment features ever assembled." The image above shows the Deep Sea Aquarium with a wide array of ocean creatures on display. On the roof of the aquarium is a giant reclining figure of Neptune. The Roman god of the sea, made of plaster, was recycled from a float used in the expo's ground-breaking parade. The postcard below shows the entrance to Thompson's Scenic Railway (an early roller coaster) on the right with the carousel building on the left. This is not the same carousel that is currently in Balboa Park. After the exposition ended on January 1, 1917, the Isthmus was dismantled, but it was brought back as the Zocalo Midway 20 years later for the California Pacific International Exposition. Today, this area is the parking lot for the San Diego Zoo.

LA JOLLA BATH HOUSE. This c. 1910 postcard shows the second bathhouse that was built above La Jolla Cove in 1906. The original 1894 bathhouse burned to the ground in 1905 due to a kitchen fire. This larger replacement bathhouse was designed by Irving Gill. The new facility overlooking the cove became a popular spot for dancing and dining. In addition to 180 dressing rooms and lockers, the bathhouse had a bowling alley, auditorium, and swimming pool. In 1925, the building was torn down after complaints that it had become an unsanitary eyesore.

GRAPE DAY FESTIVAL. Escondido attracted visitors from all over Southern California to celebrate its rich agricultural heritage at the Grape Day Festival. The festival started in 1908 and ran until 1950. This 1914 postcard shows some of the crowds and vehicles taking part in the festivities. Grape Day Park continues this tradition as the location for Escondido's community events. The historic park contains a Santa Fe Railroad depot, a working barn, a blacksmith shop, and museums.

HILLCREST BOWL. Built and operated by Wesley Whitson, the Hillcrest Bowl at 515 Washington Street had 16 lanes, and this c. 1943 postcard promised 16 additional lanes "when war conditions permit." The postcard also called the Streamline Moderne facility "the finest Bowling installation in all the west" and boasted about its unique lounge, unusual murals, milk bar that served excellent food, and parking for 250 cars. The Village Hillcrest shopping center now occupies this site.

GEORGE'S. This restaurant, like many roadside businesses of the day, was not shy about its use of signage. There was no way to miss the eight-foot-high letters seen in this c. 1935 postcard. George's was established in 1916 and was located on coastal Highway 101 in Cardiff by the Sea, a beach community that is part of the city of Encinitas. In 2023, the site is home to a Chart House restaurant.

Eight

LOST BUILDINGS

793 – State Normal School, San Diego, California.

STATE NORMAL SCHOOL. The previous chapters featured many San Diego County buildings that have been lost. This chapter focuses on the buildings that, if they stood today, would be among the region's most cherished landmarks, such as the State Normal School (above). San Diego State University can trace its beginnings to the State Normal School, first located at downtown's George Hill Building in 1898 before moving to University Heights at the corner of Park Boulevard and Normal Street. Designed in the Beaux-Arts style by William Hebbard and Irving Gill, the design borrowed heavily from the Art Palace at the 1893 Chicago World's Fair. In 1928, the school was used for Horace Mann Junior High and administrative offices. In 1955, this elegant building was unceremoniously demolished by the San Diego Unified School District, and mundane new buildings were erected for its education center headquarters.

COUNTY COURT HOUSE. The 1889 San Diego County Court House was located on D Street (Broadway) between Front and Union Streets on land donated by Alonzo Horton. The Italian Renaissance–style building included a bell and clock tower topped by a 10-foot gilded statue of Lady Justice. The courthouse had three courtrooms and a jail, featured hand-painted frescos and stained-glass windows, and reached a height of 126 feet. The stately building was demolished in 1959 for a new, modernist county courthouse. Lady Justice was salvaged and is now displayed at the San Diego History Center.

CARNEGIE LIBRARY. Industrialist turned philanthropist Andrew Carnegie funded the construction of 1,689 libraries across the United States between 1883 and 1929. In 1897, Lydia Horton, wife of Alonzo Horton, contacted Carnegie to help sponsor a library for San Diego. Carnegie donated $60,000, providing San Diego with the first Carnegie library west of the Mississippi River. The library opened in 1902 at Eighth and E Streets. Charles Lindbergh used the resources at the library to plot the course for his historic 1927 solo flight across the Atlantic Ocean. San Diego's Carnegie library was demolished in 1952 to make room for a larger library on the same site.

Union Depot, San Diego, Cal.—8

SAN DIEGO DEPOT. The Union Depot in downtown San Diego officially opened on March 8, 1915, to accommodate visitors to the Panama-California Exposition. The train station, now called the Santa Fe Depot, remains a functioning station in 2023, but it has lost the beautiful open-air forecourt on D Street (Broadway) that can be seen in these old postcards. The Spanish Colonial Revival–style station was designed by San Francisco architects Bakewell and Brown and is listed in the National Register of Historic Places. The forecourt, or patio, which once served as a streetcar stop, was demolished in 1954 to make room for a parking lot. The area is now a public plaza. The north end of the depot (above, far right) was originally used for baggage storage. In 2007, the Museum of Contemporary Art San Diego moved into the old baggage room and built a three-story addition for exhibit space and offices. Of the 73 California Amtrak stations, San Diego's Santa Fe Depot is the third busiest, serving almost 2,000 passengers per day.

4568. PATIO, SANTA FE DEPOT, SAN DIEGO, CAL.

PANTAGES THEATRE. The 1924 Commonwealth Building was developed by Alexander Pantages and featured his 2,000-seat Pantages Theatre for vaudeville performances. The theater was adapted to show movies when it became the RKO Orpheum in 1929. The Spanish Colonial Revival–style theater, at the corner of Fifth Avenue and B Street in downtown San Diego, had an elaborate curving marquee with "Pantages America's Finest" emblazoned in lights. The theater was demolished in 1964 for the First National Bank tower.

PARADISE VALLEY SANITARIUM. Built in 1887 by Dr. Anna M. Longshore Potts and located at Euclid and Eighth Streets in National City, the 30-room Paradise Valley Sanitarium promoted itself as "an ideal place in which to rest and obtain a health training. Fully equipped for Hydrotherapy, Electrotherapy, Phototherapy, Massage and all Physiologic Procedures." In 1904, Ellen G. White, one of the founders of the Seventh-Day Adventist Church, purchased the property for $4,000. A nurses' training school started on-site in 1909 and continued until 1966. The sanitarium buildings were demolished in 1967.

FIFTH AVE. AUTO WASH, FIFTH AND KALMIA, SAN DIEGO, CALIF.   1417-29

AUTO WASH. The Fifth Avenue Auto Wash, at the northwest corner of Fifth Avenue and Kalmia Street, opened for service in 1928. The back of this postcard reads, "This thoroughly modern auto laundry with a capacity for washing and vacuuming a car in 15 minutes, or 540 cars per day, at a minimum charge, sets a new standard for efficiency and speed. Also well equipped to render service in Lubricating, Polishing, Motor and Chassis Cleaning, Tires and Battery. There is joy in a clean car." This site now contains a five-story apartment building.

"ROUND HOUSE." This iconic structure, built in 1967, was designed by architect James Hurley and was sited immediately adjacent to Interstate 8 in La Mesa. The circular showroom was modeled after Ford's "Wonder Rotunda" at the 1964–1965 New York World's Fair. Drew Ford called it the "Roundhouse of Values," as seen in this 1973 postcard. The building not only displayed cars but also hosted proms and other community events. Despite public outcry, the iconic building was demolished in 2018 by Penske Ford. In 2023, the site is a parking lot.

SCIENCE AND EDUCATION BUILDING. This beautiful Spanish palace, designed by Carleton Winslow, was one of the temporary buildings constructed as an exhibit hall for the 1915 Panama-California Exposition in Balboa Park. This postcard shows the facade that faced the Plaza de Panama. The building was renamed the Palace of Science and Photography for the 1935 California Pacific International Exposition and was demolished in 1964 to make way for the San Diego Museum of Art's west wing and sculpture garden.

HOME ECONOMY BUILDING. This Balboa Park structure, with its ornate corner tower, was a near-mirror image of the House of Hospitality across El Prado. The 1915 Home Economy Building was repurposed for the Café of the World in 1935. Like the Science and Education Building, this temporary building was demolished in the mid-1960s. The loss of these two exposition buildings was the last straw for San Diego's burgeoning preservation community, and the Balboa Park Committee of 100 was formed to make sure that no other historic buildings were lost in Balboa Park.

4424. Front View of Southern California Counties Building, Panama-California Exposition, San Diego, Cal. 1915.

PANAMA-CALIFORNIA EXPOSITION, SAN DIEGO, CALIFORNIA, 1915

71651 SOUTHERN CALIFORNIA COUNTIES BUILDING

SOUTHERN CALIFORNIA COUNTIES BUILDING. This imposing structure, with its twin domed towers, was sponsored by the seven counties of Imperial, Los Angeles, Orange, Riverside, San Bernardino, San Diego, and Ventura for the 1915 Panama-California Exposition. The exhibits promoted the agricultural potential of Southern California, and the building was located adjacent to the Intensive Farm and citrus orchard. The image on the right shows the south entry patio with tropical plants and terra-cotta tile paving. Its design was inspired by the Convent of San Augustin in Querétaro, Mexico. After the exposition, the Southern California Counties Building was converted into the 3,000-seat Civic Auditorium. On November 25, 1925, the building was destroyed, but not by the wrecking ball. According to the *San Diego Union*, "The fire started about 7 o'clock as the auditorium was being made ready for the annual Firemen's Ball. . . . The flames shot hundreds of feet into the air and were seen in all parts of the city." In 1933, the Natural History Museum was built on this site.

W. H. Putnam's Residence. San Diego, Cal.

PUTNAM RESIDENCE. This large mansion with classical details was Henry W. Putnam's house in Florence Heights, adjacent to downtown San Diego. Putnam made his fortune in New York as an inventor. His patents included a fence barbing machine, an adjustable clothes wringer, and a wire fastener to hold corks on bottles known as the "Putnam bottle top stopper." Putnam died in 1915, but the Putnam family remained in San Diego and collected great works of art. The Putnam Collection is a mainstay at the Timken Museum of Art in Balboa Park.

U. S. Grant Residence, San Diego, Cal.

GRANT RESIDENCE. Ulysses S. Grant Jr., second son of Pres. Ulysses S. Grant, moved his family to San Diego in 1893 seeking a milder climate due to health reasons. Soon after their arrival, the family purchased a three-story Queen Anne–style mansion for $25,000. The house, seen in this c. 1915 postcard, was located at Eighth and Ash Streets on Prospect Hill. The site was considered one of the most valuable in San Diego because it had commanding views of downtown and the bay. The house came down in 1925 to make way for the El Cortez Hotel.

ELK'S CLUB. The San Diego Elk's Club Lodge was established in 1890, and the building seen here was dedicated on November 14, 1907. The lodge was located on the northwest corner of Second and D Streets (Broadway). This fraternal order was founded "to promote and practice the four cardinal virtues of Charity, Justice, Brotherly Love and Fidelity; to promote the welfare and enhance happiness of its members; to quicken the spirit of American Patriotism and cultivate good fellowship." Note the elk heads on the corners of the roof and the large stained-glass windows above the entrance. The site is now occupied by a 25-story office building.

MASONIC TEMPLE. The Freemasons are the oldest fraternal organization in the world, going back to the Middle Ages in Europe. The growth of the Masonic community in San Diego parallels the city's development. By 1910, the Scottish Rite (an offshoot of the Freemasons) outgrew a building they shared with the International Order of Oddfellows at Sixth and H (now Market) Streets. In 1912, they moved into their own newly built temple at the northwest corner of Fifth and Ash Streets, as seen in this c. 1915 postcard. A four-story office building is now on this site.

HOTEL SAN DIEGO. San Diego's namesake hotel was built in 1914 by John D. Speckels and was completed in time for the 1915 Panama-California Exposition. The six-story hotel was one of three buildings constructed by Speckels on D Street (now Broadway). The Hotel San Diego was designed by renowned architect Harrison Albright, who also designed Speckels's Union Building (1908), the Speckels Theatre (1912), and the Speckels Organ Pavilion (1915), plus the U.S. Grant Hotel (1910). This postcard proudly displays the seal of the exposition and touts the hotel's modern "fireproof" construction and views of the harbor, where guests can watch "men in hydroplanes [seaplanes] flying over the bay." In 2000, the Hotel San Diego appeared in several scenes in the Oscar-winning film *Traffic*. In 2006, despite strong local opposition and historic status, the well-known hotel was leveled by 358 pounds of explosives. The building was in the way of a new $273-million federal courthouse expansion.

SPRECKELS'S SKY SCRAPERS. The term "skyscraper" was coined in the 1880s, when the first tall buildings went up in the eastern United States. Referring to Spreckels's six-story buildings as skyscrapers was a bit of a reach in this 1913 postcard because that label was usually reserved for buildings at least 10 stories tall. The 1908 Union Building is seen in the foreground and was the third home of the *San Diego Union* newspaper. All of the buildings in this image have been torn down except for the Spreckels Theatre (second from the left).

ANNA'S ARK. The Ark, part of the Green Dragon Colony in La Jolla, was developed by Anna Held Heinrich, a former governess for the Ulysses S. Grant Jr. family. Held came to La Jolla in 1894 and began construction on various guest cottages. Held dubbed this boat-shaped residence with porthole windows The Ark. Held's guests included international elites—actresses, artists, musicians, writers, and other bohemian types. The art colony was world-renowned and was how many first learned about La Jolla. The Green Dragon Colony was demolished in 1991.

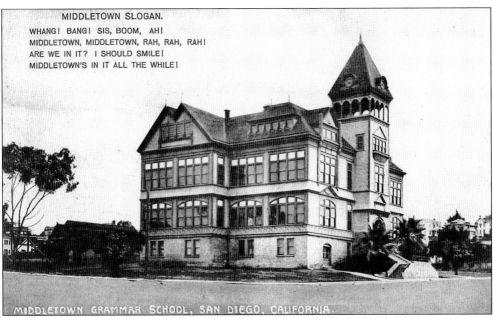

MIDDLETOWN GRAMMAR SCHOOL, SAN DIEGO, CALIFORNIA.

MIDDLETOWN SCHOOL. The Middletown Grammar School was constructed in 1888 and had 11 classrooms and a four-story bell tower. The school was located on the northwest corner of Union and Elm Streets and was one of four Victorian-era schoolhouses built during this period. This early-1900s postcard includes the school slogan. The Middletown Grammar School was demolished and replaced in 1913 by Washington Elementary.

High School Building, Escondido, California.

ESCONDIDO HIGH. This three-story brick Victorian building was located on a hill at Fourth Avenue and Hickory Street in Escondido and began in 1889 as a Methodist seminary constructed by the University of Southern California (USC). USC donated the building 10 years later, and the Escondido Union High School District turned the building into a high school. For many years, it was the only high school in the area, so many students came from the surrounding communities of San Marcos, Poway, and Valley Center. Like many old schools, the building was deemed unsafe in the event of an earthquake, so it was razed in 1954.

GREY CASTLE. Established in 1882 by Joseph Russ, San Diego High School in Balboa Park is the oldest public high school in San Diego County. This c. 1910 postcard shows the 100 Building, completed in 1907, which was nicknamed the "Grey Castle" for obvious reasons. Legislation in the 1960s required California school districts to demolish all buildings constructed prior to 1933, so San Diego High School's castle was razed and replaced with mundane new buildings in 1976.

COUNTRY CLUB. The Point Loma Country Club was built in 1914 by sporting goods magnate Albert G. Spalding, the man who also developed Sunset Cliffs Park (see page 40). The club and golf course were located across Lytton Street from the Naval Training Center in Point Loma. The golf course grounds were later sold, and the clubhouse was demolished in 1926. Funds raised by the sale of the property helped establish a new location for the club in Chula Vista under the name the San Diego Country Club.

Los Banos "The Bath House," San Diego, Cal.

LOS BANOS. Across D Street (Broadway) from the train depot, Los Banos Bath House was an architectural showcase built in the Spanish-Moorish style by famed architects William Hebbard and Irving Gill. The bathhouse, financed by Graham E. Babcock, son of Coronado developer Elisha Babcock, opened in August 1897. Admission was 25¢, which included a swimsuit, towel, and key to the locker room. The indoor, concrete "plunge tank" was 50 by 100 feet, filled with seawater, and covered by a spectacular glass roof, as seen in the postcard below. The design also included 135 dressing rooms, 25 porcelain bathtubs with shower heads, and a "Russian bath" (sauna). According to the *San Diego Union*, the facility provided "all the luxuries that a bather could desire, in the way of Turkish baths, plunges, showers, and slides." San Diego Gas and Electric Company tore down Los Banos to expand its power plant in 1928.

Interior Los Banos Bath House, San Diego, Cal.

PUBLIC MARKET. This unique-looking building with the circular tower window was located at the corner of First and A Streets in downtown San Diego. Built in the early 1900s, the City Public Market was intended to provide a fresh food shopping experience to match other large cities. The market, however, was short-lived, and the building was converted into a boxing arena, a dance hall, and a venue for evangelical revival meetings.

US NAVAL HOSPITAL. Thousands of San Diegans were brought into the world at this large medical complex in Balboa Park. Constructed in 1922, the Spanish Revival–style hospital went through many periods of expansion before the Navy decided that it needed to be replaced. This image shows a flag flying over the Administration Building, the only portion of the original hospital that was preserved. The chapel, added in 1945, now houses the Veterans Museum at Balboa Park. In 1988, a new naval medical center opened north of the original site in Florida Canyon.

HORTON PLAZA MALL. Designed by Los Angeles architect Jon Jerde, FAIA (1940–2015), this Postmodern-style shopping center transformed six and a half blocks in the center of downtown San Diego. The project was a gamble by developer Ernest Hahn (1919–1992), who was confident he could bring shoppers back downtown. Hahn once accurately described the mall as "half Disneyland, half Italian hill town." The opening festivities in August 1985 attracted 35,000 people. In its first year, 25 million shoppers and curious visitors zigzagged their way through the dynamic, colorful mall. Horton Plaza became a catalyst for downtown revitalization, including the adjacent Gaslamp Quarter, and influenced the development of similar malls throughout the world. As late as 2004, Horton Plaza continued to generate San Diego's highest retail sales per square foot. Despite its success, the mall fell victim to the great mall die-off and became a retail ghost town by 2018. In 2023, Horton Plaza mall is being heavily remodeled into the Campus @ Horton, focused on providing high-tech offices with some retail. A few features, like the triangular, tile-covered "Piazza," are being retained, but the Horton Plaza of 1985 has all but disappeared. These images were taken in 1987 by coauthor David Marshall.

Nine

ONLY IN SAN DIEGO

FROZEN. This 1913 postcard carries the caption "Once in a lifetime in San Diego" and shows a crowd at the Horton Plaza Park fountain with children standing on the frozen water. The January 6, 1913, *San Diego Tribune* reported that "the city awoke this morning in a climate apparently transplanted. Shivers ran where shivers had not run before and the weather bureau was bombarded from early morn with telephone calls to know the reason why." It did not snow, but a sudden and rare cold front blew into the city, dropping temperatures to 20 degrees, which left the fountain covered in ice.

"SUBMARINE" MOTOR CAR. William R. McKeen designed these unique gas-powered motor cars on rails that were 55 feet long and featured a pointed nose and porthole windows. Because of their odd appearance and red color, the cars were nicknamed "Submarines" and "Red Devils." In 1908, two McKeen cars were purchased by the Los Angeles & San Diego Beach Railway. Stops included Old Town, Pacific Beach, and La Jolla. The cars served until 1914. A third McKeen car was used by the San Diego & Cuyamaca Eastern Railway.

THE SCISSORS GRINDER, SAN DIEGO, CAL.

6117. COPYRIGHT, 1902, BY DETROIT PHOTOGRAPHIC CO

DAILY GRIND. An early necessary trade, scissors grinders would travel on foot or with a horse- or mule-drawn cart from town to town. They would make themselves available for homemakers to ensure that kitchen knives and scissors were well-sharpened. Tools of the trade were basic: bell, grinding wheel, some oil, and rags. Many utilized the newspaper to announce their arrival in town. This postcard is dated 1902 and was mailed in 1907.

SAN DIEGO'S
WONDERFUL
CLOCK

This wonderful clock with twenty dials, stands twenty-one feet high, and tells simultaneously the time of all nations; also the day of the week, date and month, and marks the seconds. Four of the dials are each four feet in diameter. The master clock is enclosed in plate glass, so that its every action can be seen, and the whole is illuminated every night. The clock is jeweled with tourmaline, topaz, agate and jade. The jewels and every part of this intricate mechanism was designed and made in our shop. It is the most completely jeweled, best finished and best made street clock in America, and the only clock of its kind ever built in a retail jewelry store in the world. The motive power is a 200-lb. weight, and it winds itself automatically. It took fifteen months to build, and cost about $3000 The master clock was exhibited at the State Fair in Sacramento in 1907, and awarded a gold medal.

J. JESSOP & SONS
GRANGER BLOCK
SAN DIEGO, CALIFORNIA

MANUFACTURED BY
J. JESSOP & SONS

JESSOP'S CLOCK. Standing 22 feet tall, this elaborate street clock was built in 1907 by J. Jessop & Sons jewelers and was, according to Jessop's, "the most completely jeweled, best finished and best made street clock in America." Prior to its street installation, the clock was exhibited at the Sacramento State Fair and won a gold medal. Built by Claude Ledger, Jessop's first employee outside of the family, the clock displays the time in 12 cities around the world. Many of the jewels used for the timepiece came from Jessop's mine on Mount Palomar. The clock was originally installed on the sidewalk in front of the J. Jessop jewelry store at 952 Fifth Street. In 1985, the street clock was moved to the main level of Horton Plaza mall, where it stood next to the relocated J. Jessop & Sons jewelers. In 2023, the Jessop street clock sits in storage, but there are plans to install the clock inside the San Diego History Center's museum.

BOUNDARY MONUMENT. Stone border obelisks marked the boundary between the United States and Mexico in the years before steel fences and barbed wire became the norm. These boundary monuments were established in 1849 after the Treaty of Guadalupe Hidalgo ended the war between the United States and Mexico. The treaty resulted in Mexico ceding 55 percent of its territory, including California. One year later, California became the 31st state. This 1914 postcard shows one of the boundary monuments near "Tia Juana" (Tijuana).

RETURNING BACK TO THE STATES AFTER VISITING TIJUANA, MEXICO.   7

BORDER CROSSING. The United States began to better define its southern border with Mexico in the mid-1860s. By the 1920s and 1930s, a dramatic growth in gambling and entertainment sectors in Tijuana, Mexico, emerged. American tourists visiting San Diego often traveled through San Ysidro to Tijuana as part of their vacation. Traffic along the border crossing at this time had grown, and by 1933, twenty-four-hour operations began at the port of entry. This postcard depicts the Tijuana crossing in the 1940s.

KGB CHICKEN. The San Diego Chicken hatched in 1974 as a radio mascot for rock station KGB-FM. Inside the colorful fowl was Ted Giannoulas, who got the gig with no formal audition or interview. At the ballpark, Giannoulas entertained fans with humorous antics, and his popularity soared. Famously fired by KGB over a contract dispute, the Chicken rehatched his career as a freelance fowl in 1979 and has made over 5,100 appearances. In 1999, the Chicken faced yet another legal challenge after being sued for beating up Barney the Dinosaur in a popular skit. The Chicken won that lawsuit too and is now nesting comfortably in retirement in San Diego.

CARLSBAD CHICKEN. The KGB Chicken was not the first oversized fowl in San Diego County. This 1929 postcard shows a large chicken statue surrounded by chicks to promote the "real" fried chicken served at the Twin Inns Restaurant in Carlsbad. Built by the "Father of Carlsbad," Gerhard Schutte, this 1887 Victorian inn was converted into a restaurant that was frequented by Hollywood celebrities such as John Wayne who stopped by on their way to the Del Mar racetrack. The building on Carlsbad Boulevard remains in 2023 and is the location of the Sun Diego Boardshop—where surfboards have replaced chickens.

725:—SERRA PALM, THE FIRST PALM TREE IN CALIFORNIA. PLANTED 1769

BY THE FRANCISCAN FATHERS, OLD TOWN, SAN DIEGO, CALIF. 42400

SERRA PALM. The back of this 1940s postcard reads, "The Serra Palm, oldest Palm in California was planted by the Franciscan Fathers in 1769. It marks the burial place of more than 60 victims of scurvy from ships of the Galvey Expedition in 1769." The famous "El Camino Real" trail begins at this site. The palm tree is now gone, but a plaque on Taylor Street marks the Serra Palm Site as California Registered Landmark No. 67. The debate regarding whether palms are true trees still rages. The consensus seems to be that palms are considered trees if they grow more than 20 feet tall.

GRUNION RUN ALONG THE SOUTHERN CALIFORNIA COAST.   GW 16

GRUNION RUN. FROM March through August each year, millions of writhing silver fish appear on Southern California's beaches four nights in a row during high tides at full and new moons. The special nights they appear are called "grunion runs," and the event became a popular excuse for beach parties in San Diego, especially from the 1960s through the 1980s. The only legal way to catch grunion was by hand, so it became a slippery game. Grunion runs still occur, but they are not the social phenomenon they were a few decades ago. Mission Bay High School's own Frank Zappa wrote an instrumental song called "Grunion Run" in 1963.

The Tower,
East San Diego, Cal.

TOWER REALTY. Located in what used to be called "East San Diego" at the corner of University Avenue and Fairmont Avenue, this unique Craftsman-style lookout tower was constructed around 1910 to promote development in the area. It was originally open air but was later enclosed and housed the branch office of Columbia Realty Company. Later the structure was occupied by Tower Realty Company, as seen in this postcard. Unfortunately, this quirky landmark was razed in the 1980s.

BIG FLOOD. In late 1915, after experiencing four years of drought, the San Diego City Council agreed to pay legendary "Rainmaker" Charles Hatfield $10,000 to trigger enough rain to fill Lake Morena. In January 1916, Hatfield built a wood tower to release his secret mix of chemicals to coax water from the heavens. Weeks later, the rains came in torrents until Lower Otay Dam collapsed, sending waves crashing through low-lying communities. The postcard above depicts the San Diego River overflowing during the infamous 1916 flood. Considered the worst natural disaster in San Diego's history, the rains lasted two weeks. The "Boat Ride up C Street" postcard below shows the five feet of water that reached downtown San Diego. The flood was reported to have caused at least 20 deaths along with many bridges, buildings, roads, and rail lines washed away. Hatfield tried to collect his $10,000, but the city council would only pay Hatfield if he accepted liability for $3.5 million in damages. Hatfield sued the city, and the case was not decided until 1938. Two courts found that the rain was an act of God, which absolved Hatfield of liability but also meant he was not responsible for making the rain and would not be paid.

FIRST BRICK HOUSE IN CALIFORNIA, NEAR RAMONA'S MARRIAGE PLACE.

WHALEY HOUSE. This two-story Greek Revival–style residence was the home of Thomas Whaley and was constructed in 1857 using bricks from Whaley's own brickyard. In addition to being the Whaley family's residence, the building was a general store, was San Diego's first commercial theater, and served as the county courthouse until 1871. This postcard shows the house in 1910 before the continuous front porch and balcony were reconstructed. After a series of long-ago deaths and repeated ghost sightings, the Whaley House has become known as "America's most haunted house" and remains a popular tourist destination.

LITTLE PHILOSOPHERS. The International Theosophical Headquarters was located in Point Loma and became known as Lomaland. Construction began in 1897 and included a school, cultural center, and residential facilities. This postcard shows the "Little Philosophers" of the Raja-Yoga Academy, who learned music, drama, and military drills. Point Loma Nazarene University now occupies this site, and several of the Lomaland buildings remain, including the first Greek theater constructed in North America.

SPIRAL RAMP. This tour-de-force, high-tech interior was at the General Dynamics–Convair facility, built in 1958 in Kearny Mesa. The back of this postcard reads, "Spiral ramp suspended on aluminum rods above [a] pool dominates [the] reception center at the new $40,000,000 plant." The impressive lobby represented forward-thinking, space-age engineering and was intended to impress clients as well as potential engineers whom the company might hire. Renowned architects William Pereira and Charles Luckman designed the floating ramp and the rest of the expansive campus. Pereira is most well known for designing the Transamerica Pyramid in San Francisco (1972) and the famed UC San Diego library (1970). General Dynamics acquired Convair in 1953 and produced the Atlas intercontinental ballistic missile for the Air Force. In the early 1960s, the missile evolved to become the launch vehicle for NASA's Project Mercury, transporting men into space. General Dynamics closed its complex in Kearny Mesa, and the facility was gone by 1997. The site is now mostly houses and offices.

SUNNY JIM CAVE. The seven caves of La Jolla are located on the cliffs below Prospect Street. One of the caves can be accessed from the land side. Sunny Jim Cave was named by *The Wizard of Oz* author Frank Baum because the cave mouth reminded him of the pointy-nosed mascot of a British cereal. The cave tunnel was dug in 1902–1903 by two Chinese laborers who were hired by German-born painter and engineer Gustauf Schultz to create the tourist attraction. Although the cave may be unknown or forgotten for many San Diegans, one can still visit the Cave Store and walk down 145 steps to see a unique view of the ocean.

AT THE SAN DIEGO PANAMA-CALIFORNIA EXPOSITION ALL THE YEAR 1915

COPYRIGHT 1914, P-C-EX.   IN SAN DIEGO'S BACK COUNTRY: THE WORLD'S BEST COTTON

COTTON FIELDS. People do not usually associate Southern California with cotton fields, but this postcard features cotton being harvested in Imperial Valley. The 1915 Panama-California Exposition promoted Southern California as an agricultural paradise where anything could grow. As early as 1909, newspaper headlines boasted, "Reclaimed Desert Gives to Southern California Opportunity. First Year's Cotton Crop Establishes a New Industry and Justifies Enthusiasm." By 1918, Imperial Valley's cotton production was at its peak, but by 2008, pest infestations, fuel costs, and water rationing all but ended cotton farming in the region.

PRESIDENTIAL VISIT. US president Franklin D. Roosevelt and First Lady Eleanor Roosevelt visited San Diego in October 1935. "You have given me a wonderful party today, and I am very grateful." Those were FDR's closing words as he addressed a crowd of 60,000 at Balboa Stadium after a tour of the city. The first couple stopped at the Hotel del Coronado, the Naval Training Center, the Marine Corps Recruit Depot, and the California Pacific International Exposition in Balboa Park, where they had lunch at the House of Hospitality.

DOUBLE DECKER. The double-deck electric streetcar in this c. 1910 postcard is stopped at Coronado's Tent City. The Coronado Beach Railroad Company was established in 1886. Horse cars were used briefly and were replaced by steam-operated trains. Parts of the line were electrified in 1893. In 1908, the line was sold to the San Diego Electric Railway Company, which was owned by developer and entrepreneur John D. Spreckels. The double-decker car made its inaugural run in 1892 and was the first such electrically operated car in the United States.

BIBLIOGRAPHY

archive.org

calisphere.org

Carlin, Katherine Eitzen, and Ray Brandes. *Coronado The Enchanted Island.* Coronado, CA: Coronado Historical Association, 1998.

coronadohistory.org

co.seneca.ny.us

Donaldson, Milford Wayne, FAIA. "Architectural Conservation Assessment Program: Heritage Walk Historic Grape Day Park." Prepared for Escondido Historical Society, August 29, 1996.

———. "Heritage Walk Historic Grape Day Park." Prepared for Escondido Historical Society, August 29, 1996.

———. "Naval Training Center San Diego Guidelines for the Treatment of Historic Properties." Prepared for City of San Diego, 2000.

Engstrand, Iris, and Cynthia Davalos. *San Diego Yacht Club: A History, 1886–2000.* San Diego, CA: San Diego Yacht Club, 2000.

Heritage Architecture & Planning. "Historical Resource Research Report, Balboa Park Carousel." Prepared for Forever Balboa Park, June 2020.

———. "San Diego Stadium, 9449 Friars Road, San Diego, CA 92108 Historical Resource Technical Report." Prepared for the City of San Diego and Dyette & Bhatia, July 31, 2015.

lajollahistory.org

lamesahistory.com

oceansidechamber.com

oceansidehistoricalsociety.org

Pourade, Richard. *The History of San Diego.* 7 vols. San Diego, CA: Union-Tribune Publishing Company, 1960–1977.

sandiegoairandspace.org

sandiego.gov

sandiegohistory.org

sandiegoyesterday.com

sandiegouniontribune.newsbank.com

Scott, Mary. *San Diego Air Capital of the West.* Virginia Beach, VA: The Donning Company, 1991.

sdpl.idm.oclc.org

sohosandiego.org

Sudsbury, Elretta. *Jackrabbits to Jets: The History of North Island, San Diego, California.* San Diego: Neyenesch Printers, Inc., 1967.

DISCOVER THOUSANDS OF LOCAL HISTORY BOOKS
FEATURING MILLIONS OF VINTAGE IMAGES

Arcadia Publishing, the leading local history publisher in the United States, is committed to making history accessible and meaningful through publishing books that celebrate and preserve the heritage of America's people and places.

Find more books like this at
www.arcadiapublishing.com

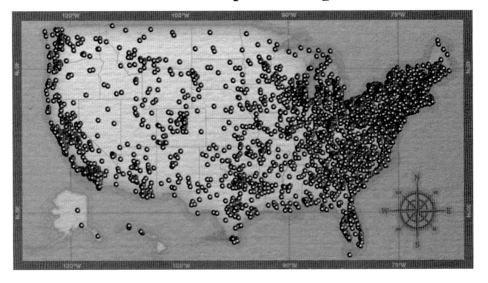

Search for your hometown history, your old stomping grounds, and even your favorite sports team.

Consistent with our mission to preserve history on a local level, this book was printed in South Carolina on American-made paper and manufactured entirely in the United States. Products carrying the accredited Forest Stewardship Council (FSC) label are printed on 100 percent FSC-certified paper.

MADE IN THE USA